INSPIRED BY TOZER

59 Artists, Writers and Leaders
Share the Insight and Passion
They've Gained from A.W. Tozer

LAUREN BARLOW

GENERAL EDITOR

Regal

From Gospel Light
Ventura, California, U.S.A.

Published by Regal
From Gospel Light
Ventura, California, U.S.A.
www.regalbooks.com
Printed in the U.S.A.

Library of Congress Cataloging-in-Publication Data
Inspired by Tozer : 50 artists, writers and leaders share the insights and passion they've
gained from A.W. Tozer / Lauren Barlow, general editor.
p. cm.
ISBN 978-0-8307-5929-3 (hard cover) —
ISBN 978-0-8307-6253-8 (international trade paper)
1. Tozer, A. W. (Aiden Wilson), 1897-1963—Influence. 2. Christian and Missionary
Alliance—United States—Clergy—Miscellanea. I. Barlow, Lauren.
BX6700.Z8T695 2011
289.9—dc23
2011035360

Rights for publishing this book outside the U.S.A. or in non-English languages are ad-
ministered by Gospel Light Worldwide, an international not-for-profit ministry. For additional information, please visit www.glww.org, email info@glww.org, or write to Gospel
Light Worldwide, 1957 Eastman Avenue, Ventura, CA 93003, U.S.A.

To order copies of this book and other Regal products in bulk quantities,
please contact us at 1-800-446-7735.

CONTENTS

INTRODUCTION

A. W. Tozer was a man of many achievements and passions. Some might say he was a bit overcommitted, but others would argue his impact on this world in all he did was worth that sacrifice. Tozer's real strength came from his prayer life. He often commented, "As a man prays, so is he." His entire ministry of preaching and writing flowed out of fervent prayer. What he discovered in prayer soon found expression in sermons, articles, editorials, books and spiritual mentorship. For his extensive work, he received two honorary doctorate degrees.

In 1919, five years after his conversion and without formal theological training, Tozer began 44 years of ministry with the Christian and Missionary Alliance. For 31 of those years, he gained prominence as pastor of Southside Alliance Church in Chicago, serving there from 1928 to 1959. During his time there, he was also editor of *The Alliance Weekly*, the official publication of the Christian and Missionary Alliance denomination. Under Tozer's leadership, the magazine's circulation doubled. During his later years (1951-1959), WMBI—the Moody Bible Institute radio station—broadcast a weekly program, *Talks from a Pastor's Study*, originating in Tozer's study at Southside Alliance. Of course, during all this time he was preaching at most of the major Bible conferences in the country and writing books.

Of the 40 books that he wrote in his lifetime, two have become classics: *The Pursuit of God* and *The Knowledge of the Holy*. His legacy continues to grow, because half a century after his death, new books by A. W. Tozer—such as *The Purpose of Man* and *Experiencing the Presence of God*—are still being published. How did that happen? James Snyder, the official biographer of Tozer, came upon about 600 previously un-transcribed audiocassettes of Tozer teaching. Working with Tozer expert David Fessenden, James vetted the tapes, mining fresh material, and Regal Books agreed to publish the new manuscripts. Regal's editors even started putting Tozer quotes on Twitter, and as of the printing of this book, he has more than 60,000 followers.

More and more people are following and re-tweeting his words; people such as Francis Chan, David Platt and Louie Giglio have quoted him in their writings; and Tozer's own books continue to appear on best-seller lists. Although A. W. Tozer died in 1963, his spiritual legacy continues to satiate those thirsty for the deep things of God. Many who are familiar with the writings of A. W. Tozer know little about the man behind the books. Even during his lifetime, most people respected him, but few knew him with any degree of intimacy. By disposition and design, he walked alone, preferring God's fellowship to people's. His relentless pursuit of God—though not without price—accounted for his spiritual strength and has resulted in the sustained popularity of his books.

In all that Tozer did and in all that he sacrificed, his passion was to see God's people come to the desperate realization of how much we need Him—because he knew all lives were meaningless without Him. As you read through the pages of this book, may the words of this man of God make a mark in your heart.

A Passion for A. W. Tozer

LAUREN BARLOW

General Editor

In my 26 years on this earth, never once did I think I would be writing an introduction to a book. I certainly never thought I would be the editor of one. I was that sassy child in homeschool who tried convincing her mother that she didn't have to take English class because "drummers don't need to diagram sentences." Well, I have a very strong mother, so that one didn't go over so well. In retrospect, I'm glad it didn't. (But don't tell my mom I said that.)

I may not have always enjoyed the more "technical" side of grammar, but one thing that has been my obsession since I was young was my love for reading. I loved reading all sorts of books, but it was always difficult for me to dig into the more spiritual ones because it was so hard to focus. At least, that was the case until one day, about five years ago, when a friend of mine told me I needed to read A. W. Tozer's *The Pursuit of God*. I decided I'd pick up a copy—after all, it was a really thin book so it seemed painless enough. Little did I know how that book would change my spiritual life.

Words can't describe the way I felt after reading the first chapter. It was like every word and thought jumped off the page and shot like an arrow straight into my heart. I didn't skim; I dug in. This man's writing communicated such a depth and passion for the things of God. His words ignited something inside of me. His passion fed my passion. His knowledge of the things of God made me hungry to know God more in my own life. I could *feel* that everything he wrote was something he had gone through and experienced. His words reflected his life.

The other reason I knew I was going to like him so much is that I found out A. W. Tozer spent 31 years of his life in what I consider to be the best city in the world—my hometown, Chicago. He was the pastor of Southside Alliance Church in Chicago. During that time, he was also preaching at most of the major Bible conferences in the country, writing books, being the editor of a magazine and broadcasting a weekly program on the radio.

Tozer grew up in a tiny farming community in the hills of western Pennsylvania, so schooling was limited. He never had formal theological training. I find it amazing that a man who did so many incredible things never even had proper schooling. His life is evidence that God loves using the seemingly "foolish" things of the world to confound the wise.

I find it truly amazing that a man born over a century ago still changes lives today. The words he uttered were so passionate that they continue to impact society and culture. The way he spoke and challenged people is still something we all need to take to heart as believers. He was a man truly called by God, and he did whatever he could to make sure he was fulfilling that calling. His life was dedicated to God, and in my opinion he couldn't have done a better job. That is why I agreed to be a part of this wonderful book.

Honestly, when I was first asked to be the general editor of this book, I absolutely wanted to say *no!* I'm just the drummer in a rock band. Editing wasn't a talent I knew I possessed. But then I thought about it for a second. I was being offered the opportunity to be a small part of the legacy of a man who has changed millions of lives all over the world, mine included. Plus, I'm always up for a challenge and an adventure. So I said yes.

I'm honored to have the chance to introduce A. W. Tozer to people in a new way. Now, I couldn't possibly expound on all of Tozer's great quotations by myself. I knew I needed some help. So the idea was birthed to invite people who have been inspired by Tozer to contribute to this collection. Each piece starts with a Tozer quotation—some from his classics and some newly discovered ones. Then the author shares how those words have impacted him or her personally. The writers of these stories are great men and women of today. A few of them actually met Tozer or heard him speak, but all have been impacted by his life and legacy. Many of them are people whom I personally look up to—people who have helped me grow so much in my walk with God. These writers are definitely also a diverse group! They have different views on spirituality and even on the way we should live our lives.

That is what I love so much about the Body of Christ. As we were growing up, our parents exposed my siblings and me to nearly every aspect of Christianity—from the most conservative circles to the most extreme, radical ways of living out our faith. I have learned from all of it. I have heard God speak through different kinds of people and seen Him move in many ways. You can't put God in a box or say He is only present in "this or that kind of church." He moves and speaks through all of His people—the whole Church. As you read this book, whether or not you agree with a particular writer's theological background, I encourage you to listen to the stories, let them sink in, and read with an open heart. My fervent desire is that as you do so, you will experience the God Tozer spoke about with such passion and love. Much like Tozer himself, the men and women who offer reflections here have dedicated their lives to God's calling, and it's an honor to have their stories in this book. I hope and believe that Tozer would be proud.

—⊱⊰— 1 —⊱⊰—

GOD
INCOMPREHENSIBLE

CHARLES R. SWINDOLL
Author, *Insight for Living* Radio Host and
Senior Pastor, Stonebriar Community Church, Frisco, Texas

Teach us to know that we cannot know, for the things of God knoweth no man, but the Spirit of God. Let faith support us where reason fails, and we shall think because we believe, not in order that we may believe.
A. W. TOZER

Aiden Wilson Tozer died the year I began studying for the ministry. He had spent 31 years pastoring the unobtrusive Southside Alliance Church in Chicago. During his ministry, which included both the spoken and the written word, this intense, provocative man—small in stature but strong of heart—functioned as the conscience of evangelicalism. Yet, I never once heard him speak in person. Nor did most of my contemporary ministerial colleagues.

A. W. Tozer knew God and proclaimed Him fervently. "To listen to Tozer preach was as safe as opening the door of a blast furnace!" said Warren Wiersbe, aptly describing the man's style.

No, I never heard Tozer preach. Yet, in a very real sense, this great man of God lives on, influencing my life and many others, for his pen continues to punch holes in our pseudo-sophistication. It prods us awake when we would otherwise nod off into dreamland.

I haven't counted them recently, but I suppose I have in my possession a dozen or more of Tozer's tough-minded volumes that dare me to drift off course. I don't always agree with him, but he never fails to stimulate my thinking and challenge my walk with Christ. Mystical and severe though he may have been, the man asked the right questions. Questions like: *Is God real to you? Is your Christianity a set of definitions? Is it a list of orthodox doctrines, or is it a vital relationship with Christ? Is your Christianity firsthand and fresh or secondhand? Do you genuinely hunger after God?*

With daring dogmatism, the man didn't stop with casual investigation. He assaulted the status quo with insightful and relentless determination. What he lacked in humor, he made up for in zeal. It didn't take him a hundred pages to get to the point—something most of us would do well to emulate. He pounced like a hen on a June bug—and woe betide the thing within his claws! Those who respect his prophet-like call do not remain the same. *The Pursuit of God, The Divine Conquest, The Root of the Righteous* and *God Tells the Man Who Cares* continue to be some of my most treasured volumes.

With his usual, practical manner, Tozer pinpoints the awe we need to rediscover: "Teach us to know that we cannot know, for the things of God knoweth no man, but the Spirit of God. Let faith support us where reason fails, and we shall think because we believe, not in order that we may believe."[1] The psalmist is correct: The heavens *do* indeed tell of the glory of God . . . their expanse *does* indeed declare the work of His hands (see Psalm 19:1). When you mix that unfathomable fact with the incredible reality that He cares for each one of us right down to the last, tiniest detail, the psalmist is, again, correct: Such knowledge is beyond me . . . I cannot even imagine it (see Psalm 139:6).

Lost in silent solitude, I often have been impressed anew with the vast handiwork of our incomprehensible God. I find His incomprehensibility absolutely refreshing. It is delightful to be reminded that "our God is in the heavens" and that "He does whatever He pleases" (Psalm 115:3, *NASB*). He doesn't ask permission. He doesn't bother to explain. He simply does "whatever He pleases," thank you. After all, He is the Lord . . . the Maker of heaven and earth, the sovereign God of all the universe.

We need that reminder—we who are tempted to think we're capable of calling the shots. How many times must our incomprehensible God tell us that His ways are "past finding out" (Romans 11:33) before we begin to believe it? Since the Son of God found it necessary at the crossroads of His earthly existence to pray, "Not as I will, but as You will" (Matthew 26:39), we would be wise to use the same eight words often . . . every day!

One of the practical ways God's incomprehensibility works itself out is in the pain He allows into our lives. Truth be told, if there is anything that draws us close together as humans, it is this: We all hurt—some more intensely, more deeply or more profoundly than others, but we all know pain. Though we often view it as an enemy, pain is an essential part of God's inexplicable curriculum that leads to obedience.

It's a painful truth: Suffering is essential if we hope to become effective for God. God has at His disposal whatever He wishes to bring into our lives. To the surprise of those who've not stopped to think about it, among those things are suffering and pain. God wants us to be always growing—becoming whole, mature, strong and enduring. He wants us wise and deep, not silly and shallow.

A. W. Tozer was right: "It is doubtful whether God can bless a man greatly until He has hurt him deeply."[2] Solomon, in his journal named Ecclesiastes, wrote:

Consider the work of God, for who is able to straighten what He has bent? In the day of prosperity be happy, but in the day of adversity consider—God has made the one as well as the other (Ecclesiastes 7:13-14, *NASB*).

Psalm 119 echoes this same thought:

Before I was afflicted I went astray, but now I keep Your word. . . . It is good for me that I was afflicted, that I may learn Your statutes. . . . I know, O LORD, that Your judgments

are righteous, and that in faithfulness You have afflicted me
(vv. 67,71,75).

If you have reached the place in your Christian life where you
are beyond the message of today's superficial theology, you are
prepared for this truth. Feel-good, be-happy theology attempts to
understand the incomprehensible—to put God in a box. But the
pain God allows in our lives breaks the world's mold and renews
our minds according to His good pleasure.

Suffering softens our spirits and makes us sensitive to God's
voice—for He doesn't leave us alone in our pain. In the stark reality
of whatever may be the affliction, God quiets us, calms us and reminds us that everything that occurs reaches us only after being fil-
tered through His hand and permitted for His purposes and glory.

Although this journey along the avenue of affliction is unpleasant and unappealing, it is both inevitable and essential. No
one in God's family can remain a stranger to pain and suffering.
Working through the hurt is essential if we hope to become effective for God.

The more I ponder the world around us and the universe above
us—be it the starry skies, the stormy seas, the majestic mountains
or the intense suffering we endure—the more I want to pause, stand
still and let the wonder in. Why? Because that's when we see God as
who He should be to us—as who He is—namely *God incomprehensible*. Holy? Of course. Powerful? Yes, no question. Compassionate?
Absolutely. Righteous and just? Gracious, loving, self-sufficient
and sovereign? All of the above, certainly.

But He is more . . . so much more.

More than we can grasp. More than we can measure or pre-
dict. More than the brightest among us can even *imagine*.

What are the benefits of such a realization? We no longer reduce Him to manageable terms. We're no longer tempted to ma-
nipulate Him or His Word. We don't have to explain Him and His
will or defend Him and His ways. Even when those ways include
persistent pain and affliction, we acknowledge His sovereign right
to be in full control.

Our God is incomprehensible . . . yet, we long to know more about Him. The words of A. W. Tozer have provided me with a place to begin. How does one embark upon a discovery of who God is? Humbly. And with awe.

Notes

1. A. W. Tozer, *The Knowledge of the Holy: The Attributes of God: Their Meaning in the Christian Life* (San Francisco: HarperSanFrancisco, 1992), p. 9.

2. A. W. Tozer, *The Root of the Righteous* (Camp Hill, PA: Christian Publications, 1986), p. 137.

MAINTAINING A HIGH VIEW OF GOD

MIKE BICKLE
Pastor and Founder, IHOP-KC
(International House of Prayer of Kansas City)

The low view of God entertained almost universally
among Christians is the cause of a hundred lesser evils
everywhere among us. . . . A rediscovery of the majesty
of God will go a long way toward curing them.

A. W. TOZER

During the summer following my high-school graduation in the mid '70s, I served on the youth staff of a Presbyterian church in Kansas City. Our church had deep connections with Campus Crusade for Christ; youth evangelism was our heartbeat. I was 18 years old and new to ministry.

One day, the youth pastor I worked under came looking for me. "If you're going to go anywhere with God," he said, holding out a book to me, "you have to study this book." It was a little volume, *The Knowledge of the Holy*, by A. W. Tozer. My youth pastor gave me a second book as well—Leonard Ravenhill's *Why Revival Tarries*. "These books need to become a critical part of your life," he challenged me. "Okay," I told him, "if it's that important." He nodded. "It's that important."

I had never heard of A. W. Tozer or his classic book. But I loved my youth pastor, and I trusted him. So I took his counsel, and I determined on the spot that these two books would be at the top of my list. I started reading Tozer. I didn't understand all the concepts, but I was completely gripped by what he had to say about the holiness of God.

That fall, I left for the University of Missouri. I started a Bible study, and eventually 100 to 200 students were coming every Tuesday night. To prepare for the meetings, I would take the Tozer book and study it, chapter by chapter. I worked to memorize the main points, and then I'd repeat them in my Bible study. When the students asked me about the teaching, I'd tell them I got it from a man named A. W. Tozer, whom I'd only just heard of.

Tozer's book so impacted me that I became riveted to the subject of the person of God. I took on J. I. Packer's book *Knowing God*, and after that, A. W. Pink's *Gleanings in the Godhead*. Other books followed.

Of course, I also absorbed Ravenhill's *Why Revival Tarries*. Because I'd been given that book along with Tozer's, I always put the two preachers together in my mind. Many years later, when I got to know Leonard Ravenhill, I found out that he and Tozer had been good friends. I was amazed to discover how deeply Tozer had impacted Ravenhill.

But the knowledge of God's attributes was only a starting place. From there I had to turn my knowledge into prayer. My relationship with God had to be more than information I'd underlined in a book; it had to grow into a living understanding in my heart.

As I focused on God and learned to worship Him, I discovered a couple of things. I realized that the more we understand God's character—His deep love, His greatness, His ability to see everything and be very near to us—the more we want to pray. As I meditated on God's grandeur, my heart was exhilarated by His presence. I longed to be with God more and more because I was learning to be fascinated and awestruck by Him. Most people think of prayer as petition—asking God to better their circumstances. But worship—contemplating God and gazing on Him as the elders and the four living creatures and the vast multitude did in Revelation 4 and 5—is foundational to prayer.

The other thing that grew out of my contemplation of God's character was a confidence in Him that could sustain me during times of crisis. One of His attributes especially, His mercy, ministered to me when as a young man I was struggling with my sin and my lust and my failures. Realizing that God loved me—that He enjoyed me—gave me a confidence in my early days. As my confidence in God's love grew, I ran to God in my struggles instead of from Him. My loyalty to Jesus intensified. In theological debates today, many refuse to take a strong stand for Jesus as they become tolerant of other religious ideas. I cannot overemphasize the importance of loyalty to Jesus. He is God and the only way to salvation.

Worship has become a very important aspect of my prayer life. I spend more time talking to God about Himself than in any other kind of prayer. Then I pray for revival and for an outpouring of the Spirit on the Church and on our nation, and finally I make personal petition. But it all begins with a high view of God.

Our natural orientation is always toward a low view of God. When things go wrong and fear takes hold of my heart, I determine that I will not give in to my natural, automatic low view of God that weakens my desire to pursue Him and destroys my faith and confidence.

Over the years, I've told many about Tozer's little book. As my ministry grew and we began holding conferences, I would often hold up the A.W. Tozer book and tell people, "This book is a must." When I started the IHOP KC in 1999, I did the same thing. I just told people what my youth pastor had told me. We're still selling that book today.

The Knowledge of the Holy changed my life. That one-two punch I got from Tozer and Ravenhill when I was 18 formed my entire ministry. It gave me an exalted perspective of God—a God-centered orientation that is critical to sustained, effective ministry—that I never would have had otherwise.

My youth pastor was right. It was that important.

A Life of Excellence

Kurt Warner
Retired NFL Quarterback, Super Bowl Winner

Refuse to be average. Let your heart soar as high as it will.
A. W. TOZER

After an up-and-down first seven years of my NFL career, I moved to Arizona and signed with the Arizona Cardinals. The history and expectations of the franchise had been extremely dim for the last decade, and it didn't take me long to identify part of the problem. After one of my first practices with the team, I was having dinner with one of my teammates, and we began talking about different aspects of the practice. I remember giving him a few pointers I had learned over the years to help him improve his trade. He seemed only semi-interested in my comments, so I asked him what I thought was a simple question: "Don't you want to be the *best?*"

It seemed to me a rhetorical question, because as a professional player I believed there was only one possible answer. But my teammate replied in a way that shed some light on one of the underlying problems within the organization. His response to my question went something like this:

"Why? I am good enough!"

His answer surprised me, especially coming from someone performing at such a high level in his profession. But, as I have come to realize more and more over the years, I should *not* have been surprised, because this is an attitude prevalent in our society. We live in a culture where so many simply want to "get by." We subscribe to a "have our cake and eat it too" mentality—but only if it doesn't cost us too much.

After having that conversation with my teammate, I understood more fully why God had brought me to Arizona. Yes, I wanted to revitalize my career and help lead the Cardinals to on-the-field success. But more importantly, my role was to display a standard of excellence that seemed to be missing. I had been given the opportunity to demonstrate to everyone—coaches, teammates, fans and front office personnel—what it looked like to live *every day* according to this standard.

The exhortation by the great theologian A. W. Tozer is the perfect summation: "Refuse to be average. Let your heart soar as high as it will."

For me, the process began in meeting rooms and on the practice field, but it was in no way limited to just football. To live a life of excellence means striving for the same *high* standard regardless of the task you are facing. Excellence means being the best you can be in your profession, but also being the best in large and small aspects of your everyday life.

I strive to display excellence in studying the game of football, but also in being a devoted husband. I strive to display excellence in my practice habits, but also in being a hands-on dad with my seven kids. I strive to display excellence in my performance on Sunday afternoons in the stadium, but also in applying the moral principles I learn on Sunday mornings in church.

The biggest obstacle to excellence is that it isn't easy! Regardless of the task, being the best always takes work, time and sacrifice; this is likely the reason it eludes so many of us.

Over the years, I have signed thousands of autographs, and I always include a Bible verse. One of my favorites—a challenge from Paul that mirrors Tozer's quotation—is found in the book of

Colossians: "Whatever you do, work at it with all your heart, as working for the Lord" (Colossians 3:23, *NIV*).

The key word in that verse is *whatever*! It doesn't give us an excuse to slack when we are doing seemingly insignificant tasks. Character is formed every moment of our lives. When we are willing to make concessions in the smaller areas of life, that attitude almost always carries over into other areas.

I have always gravitated toward individuals, like A. W. Tozer, who display a standard of excellence in their lives. I have tried to adopt many of those standards in my own life, for I have always believed the greatest legacy I can leave my friends, teammates, fans, wife or children is to inspire them daily to want to live lives of excellence.

My wife often teases me because I don't ever put this standard on the shelf. She has witnessed me beating a pediatric hospital patient in a video game, she has ridden with me when I drove miles back to a store because they gave me too much change, and she has seen me sacrifice hours of sleep to be the best I could be when I stepped onto the football field.

If there is one thing I refuse to be, it's *average*. I want to apply a standard of excellence to *whatever* I do, because this is how I can truly represent Jesus the way He deserves to be represented.

In professing to others that I am a Christian, I believe it is my responsibility to reflect the person of Jesus Christ as best I can. As I have studied the life of Jesus, many traits have jumped off the pages, but one that was never compromised was His commitment to excellence. Jesus *always* "refused to be average and let His heart soar" to the highest of standards. I want others to be able to say the same about me.

After deciding to retire from the NFL after 12 amazing seasons, I sat down with the same teammate I mentioned earlier. We spoke of a lot of the experiences we had shared—from the Super Bowl, to inside jokes, to the numerous trips over the years. But, even with all those amazing moments, there was one comment within the conversation that stays etched in my memory and inspires me daily as I move on to accomplish new things for Jesus.

Toward the end of our conversation, my friend turned to me and said, "You have taught me many things over the years, but the one thing I will never forget about you is how *you made me want to be the best I could be* in every area of my life!"

I know I am a long way from being perfect, but to me being a Christian means striving every day to represent Jesus by being your *best*! It means "refusing to be average, and letting your heart soar as high as it will."

IF WE WOULD
REMEMBER . . .

BIANCA JUAREZ
Bible Teacher, Speaker and Founder,
In the Name of Love Ministries

Oh, if we would only remember who God is!
A. W. TOZER

The edge of the bed was the only stable item in a room that was spinning. I felt short of breath, and the walls of my mind were caving in. On the day I was supposed to be celebrating my twenty-first year of life, I sat on my dorm room bed and felt everything *but* celebratory.

Oh . . .

"Oh," I numbly replied to my father, who waited on the other end of the phone. *Oh* was the only word to fall off my lips. *Oh* was the only word I could say. *Oh* was the only word I felt. My mother was diagnosed with not one, but two forms of cancer on my twenty-first birthday. It was an unnecessary, unwanted birthday gift wrapped in ugly paper.

Oh, if . . .

If it hadn't been finals week, I would've driven to the hospital. If I hadn't been in a dysfunctional, broken relationship, I would've called my boyfriend. If I wasn't feeling anesthetized to life, I would've cried. But I didn't. I sat on a stiff college bed and felt nothing, not even an urge to breathe.

Oh, if we . . .

We had been through so much as a family—but even in financial poverty, God had never let us down. In losses of job, house and car, my father ingrained in us the belief that God would provide. In times of confusion, we were instructed to trust the Lord for direction. In times of plenty, we knew that God was the giver of all, and we owed gratitude to our provider. Now in times of illness I found myself asking, "What if?"

Oh, if we would . . .

Would God take Mom from Daddy? From us? From the church? Would God disappoint the hopes, wishes and prayers from people at our church who *needed* their pastor's wife? Would God forget how she sacrificed for Him, for us, for them? Would God even care?

Oh, if we would only remember . . .

Remembering God's past kindnesses was the last thing on my mind in those first moments after I hung up the phone. Instead, I fell to my knees, and then on my face. Then I curled into a fetal position, overwhelmed by the unanswerable questions. I wept uncontrollably—my tears bitter and my anger at the silence intense. When the anger finally melted, and my cold heart softened, I remembered. I remembered the donated food on our porch when Daddy lost his job. I remembered the car a church friend lent us. I remembered the fact that though my boyfriend didn't love me, God did. I remembered the Red Sea, the manna, the cloud and the pillar of fire. I remembered the fish and loaves, the water and wine, the blind and the sick. I remembered who God said He was.

Oh, if we would only remember who . . .

"Who do you say I am?" Jesus asked this question of His disciples throughout the Gospels, and I had also heard it on the floor of Harris Hall, my college dorm. "Who do you say I am?"

Oh, if we would only remember who God . . .

God—the Alpha and Omega, the beginning and the end, the giver and taker of life. God—the creator of all, the sustainer of all, the lover of all. God—the author, editor and finisher of our faith. God—the first, the last, the eternal. God—caller, listener, speaker. God—healer, rebuilder, restorer. God who loved Adam, loved Esau, loved Judas, loves me. God—almighty, all-powerful, all-knowing. God. God and nothing else.

Oh, if we would only remember who God is!

EXPERIENCING
HIS PRESENCE

STAN JANTZ
Co-author of the Bestselling *God Is in the Small Stuff*
and More than 50 Books

*Start the day seeking God's presence and search
for Him all through the day and revel in the gracious
encounters of God throughout the day.*
A. W. TOZER

I met A. W. Tozer for the first and last time when I was four years old. I don't remember much about that day—except that my father was dying, and Dr. Tozer was his only hope.

My father grew up in a Christian and Missionary Alliance church in a small town in Minnesota. He married his high school sweetheart, attended a Bible college in St. Paul, and then moved with my mother and me to a Chicago suburb so he could continue his studies at Wheaton College. During this time, before his twenty-fifth birthday, my father was diagnosed with Hodgkins disease. Today this form of cancer is highly treatable if detected early. In the mid-1950s there was little hope for survival. Still, my father held out hope. He served a mighty God and believed God could and would heal him. But he needed someone to pray for his healing. That's when Dr. Tozer came into our lives.

For more than 30 years, A. W. Tozer served as the pastor of Southside Alliance Church in Chicago. Though he had no formal theological training, he was known as a man whose deep heart for God was wedded to a keen mind. Our family attended Southside, so Dr. Tozer was our pastor—a fact lost on me, but of great significance to my father. When it became clear that there was no medical answer for his grave condition, my father asked Dr. Tozer to come to pray for his healing.

Within a few months, my father passed from this life into the presence of God, an event that profoundly affected my mother and me. Yes, there was pain—deep pain and sorrow—yet there was also healing, something I have come to understand in the years since.

Physically, my father wasn't healed, but that doesn't mean Dr. Tozer's prayer was ineffective, or that God somehow dropped the ball. Our primary desire in these kinds of life-and-death situations is always for physical healing, and sometimes this happens. But God's overwhelming desire is for our spiritual healing, and in this sense Dr. Tozer's prayer was highly effective.

Although he would soon die physically, my father was healed spiritually on the day Dr. Tozer prayed for him. Within a short time, my father was enjoying what Tozer often referred to as "the manifest presence of God." Of course, experiencing God in this way is something every Christian can anticipate, but we don't have to wait until we are in heaven to come into the presence of the One who loves us more deeply and knows us more intimately than we could ever imagine.

Dr. Tozer believed that "the heart of man truly hungers for God's presence." Although my father's hunger was long ago satisfied once and for all, I have the opportunity each day to enter into God's presence—and so do you—thanks to the person and work of Christ.

I am grateful for the connection that I have to two men who knew what it was like to experience God's presence in a profound way on earth, and who are now basking in His glory in heaven. Even more, I am thankful that whether I live or die, I belong to the Lord and can truly revel in those gracious encounters of God each and every day.

DARING
TO LISTEN

LISA BEVERE
International Speaker, Bestselling Author and
Co-host of *The Messenger* Television Program

*If you do all the talking when you pray,
how will you ever hear God's answers?*
A. W. TOZER

I love this timeless challenge to our prayer lives. But tragically
the answer to Tozer's question is that we won't—and sadly, too
often we don't! If ever there was a time not only to pray, but also
to hear God's response, that time is now! If we truly believe
prayer is a dialogue rather than a religious monologue, we will
allow for the rhythm of conversation. On these pages, I want to
lend context and propose three reasons we may not wait in His
presence to hear—and make some suggestions about how we can
change this.

Pausing to listen requires a posture of stillness and an investment of time. It also places a demand on our measures of faith,
hope and love. *Faith* believes that God not only hears our spoken
words but also goes beyond this and answers the deepest, un-
voiced longings of our hearts. The quickening of faith gives God
some substance to work with.

And it is impossible to please God without faith. Anyone who wants to come to him must believe that God exists and that he rewards those who sincerely seek him (Hebrews 11:6, *NLT*).

I am honored to have grandchildren. When they so much as smile in my direction, they get a response from me. They believe their G-mama will respond to all of their requests. How much more will our heavenly Father, the grandest of all parents, do so for us? He is, after all, able to do far more than any of us can dream.

This overarching *hope* creates an expectancy that anchors our lives to the provision of heaven, which is independent of our current circumstances. This allows *love* to wrap us in the wonder of a Father God who answers us, not according to our limited perspective of language, but from His vast wisdom, vantage and great love for us.

Having framed this context, I must say that I understand how daunting the silence of listening can be. I propose that the first reason we don't listen for what God has to say is that *we are afraid He won't speak to us*. We've all thought, "If I am silent and *He is silent*, does that mean my voice went unheard?" So we fill any void with our words or hurriedly close the prayer time before our hope can be disappointed.

Here's a perspective on prayer that helped me make the change: *God longs to speak to you more than you want to hear from Him, and you need to hear from Him more than He needs to hear from you.*

We can release a thousand words into the atmosphere and yet remain unchanged, but when He speaks one word to our hearts, we are transformed. Settle it: He wants to speak into your life and give you the answers and insights you need. One of God's greatest invitations is found in Jeremiah:

Ask me and I will tell you remarkable secrets you do not know about things to come (Jeremiah 33:3, *NLT*).

If we ask, He will tell.

The second reason we may not wait or listen for His response is that *we don't want to hear* what He might speak. Perhaps we're afraid He'll condemn us, or maybe our hearts already accuse us. We know we are asking amiss, but don't want to deal with the heart attitude that causes this. Or it may be that we've lost or never had the confidence of coming into His presence. If we pray out of fear or duty, then sin or shame muffles our hearing. We will hide our lack of obedience or uncomfortable feelings with busyness. No matter what the root cause, fear and disobedience will always distort our perception of God and twist how we hear Him.

Here's the great news: Even when we mess up (and who doesn't?), if we repent, our ears are opened and our lives turn around.

So let us come boldly to the throne of our gracious God. There we will receive his mercy, and we will find grace to help us when we need it most (Hebrews 4:16, *NLT*).

God corrects those He loves and comforts all who come to Him with an open heart. I believe God is always speaking, even in His silence. Sometimes there is a necessary time of waiting on the impartation of peace and rest.

Here's what I want you to do: Find a quiet, secluded place so you won't be tempted to role-play before God. Just be there as simply and honestly as you can manage. The focus will shift from you to God, and you will begin to sense his grace (Matthew 6:6, *THE MESSAGE*).

This brings us to the last reason I want to highlight: *We are too busy to listen.* I know this is the one I am guilty of most often. Everyone's life is full, but that doesn't mean we should allow the demands of our schedules to drive us from His presence. In our day and age, it requires an intentional effort to hear from God.

Phones, emails and social networks must be shut down so we can hear Him. When we close our eyes, we are suddenly separated from the seen, so our focus can shift to the eternal. We desperately need God's answers. Our world is in a season of such upheaval and injustice that God alone holds the answers. We all need to hear from heaven, receive God's directives, and then begin to express His answers through the actions of our lives. Press in boldly, and never doubt that God wants to awe you with His voice and counsel.

DISTINGUISHED BY HIS PRESENCE

BILL JOHNSON
Author and Senior Pastor, Bethel Church, Redding, California

*How many Christians really harbor within their own spirit the
daily expectation of God's presence?*
A. W. TOZER

When I married my wife, I was not interested in the philosophy or concept of marriage alone. The marriage license has importance, but it means little if there isn't a relationship to illustrate its meaning. It's the ongoing relationship, built through encounters, that makes a marriage. So it is with our relationship with God.

For many, the idea of God's abiding presence has been reduced to a doctrine or a concept, not an ongoing experience. We know that He is with us because He said so in His Word—and that's a good place to start. But the doctrine is an invitation to an encounter—and that encounter is the beginning place of a relationship. A. W. Tozer knew this reality, and he challenged the people of God into the discovery of the greatest of all realities: God's abiding presence.

God spoke often in the Scriptures to people about His commitment to them. He frequently crowned that expression with the promise that He would be with them. Every time God gave this promise, it was because He had just given an individual or a group an impossible assignment. For example, Joshua had to fill the shoes of the man who had met with God face to face; further, he was charged with successfully leading Israel into the Promised Land: something Moses had failed to do. Fearful Gideon had to rise to his calling and lead Israel out of idolatry and into a military triumph over their enemies. On and on it goes—impossibilities become possible when God is with His people. A perusal of Scripture quickly makes it apparent that His abiding presence was the perfect opportunity for men and women to know God—and out of that relationship was to come the courage, strength, faith and purpose needed for their lives.

When God revealed Himself as Jehovah Jireh to Abraham, He was not trying to round out Abraham's theological understanding of God's nature as a provider. He was trying to draw Abraham into an experience through which he realized firsthand that God is the one who provides. In that moment, Abraham looked up the hill, saw a ram caught in a bush and discovered that God provides— and not only that, but also that He *is* the Provider. An encounter with the Provider brought provision. So it is with every revelation of God: It is an invitation to discover Him through encounter and experience. Such a discovery invites interaction, co-laboring and partnership.

This great privilege of hosting the presence of our Creator is beyond comprehension. Yet it is that reality that separates God's people from every other group on the planet. Israel discovered this uniqueness in Moses' famous dialogue with God in Exodus 33:16: "For how then can it be known that I have found favor in Your sight, I and Your people? Is it not by Your going with us, so that we, I and Your people, may be distinguished from all the other people who are upon the face of the earth?" (*NASB*). In this context, He is what distinguishes us from all other people.

The revelation of God's abiding presence must be discovered daily. He is to be realized, treasured and celebrated. For in this great privilege of hosting the abiding presence of God is found the ability to do the impossible assignment given to us: "Go therefore and make disciples of all the nations, baptizing them in the name of the Father and the Son and the Holy Spirit, teaching them to observe all that I commanded you; and lo, I am with you always, even to the end of the age" (Matthew 28:19-20, *NASB*). To ensure that we maintain courage and focus, God once again promises, "I am with you, even to the end of the age."

8

MERCY TRIUMPHS OVER JUDGMENT

NANCY ALCORN
Founder and President, Mercy Ministries

Mercy is not something God has but something that God is.
A. W. TOZER

Mercy doesn't come naturally to us; it's not who we are as humans. The typical human response to other people is judgment. God, although He judges sin, says in James 2:13 that "mercy triumphs over judgment." God *is* mercy, and this reference in James is exactly why I chose the name Mercy Ministries over 28 years ago, when I first started our outreach to troubled young women with life-controlling issues.

In the eight years I spent working for the State of Tennessee in a juvenile correctional facility for girls and investigating child abuse cases, I saw a lot of judgment. That judgment never changed anyone's life—at least, not for the better. I saw so many hurting young girls lose hope. Some of them had been damaged by years of abuse. Some of them had chosen a path of rebellion that led them into a life of captivity and darkness. What they needed was God. What they needed was a heart change that can only be experienced through the mercy of God. It was because of God's mercy that He gave His only Son to pay the price for our sin and give us freedom to choose a new beginning.

I knew back then that God was calling me to raise up homes where these girls could personally experience mercy. God showed me that in an atmosphere where a hurting young woman was loved rather than judged—where she heard about forgiveness instead of condemnation—she would choose to receive Christ and allow Him to give her a new heart and a new spirit. Then and only then would she be truly transformed.

Mercy can move mountains: mountains of doubt, pain, tragedy, bondage and fear. I've seen it thousands of times in the lives of thousands of young women who have walked through the doors of our facilities in America and other countries.

One of the best examples I have ever seen of God's mercy is with a young girl named Chris. I first met Chris over 20 years ago, when she was facing an unplanned pregnancy, had had multiple abortions, and was heavily addicted to drugs. When she learned she was pregnant again, she immediately wanted to get an abortion out of fear that the baby would be deformed. Then MERCY intervened, and God caused our paths to cross. I was able to speak to her one hour before the baby was scheduled to be aborted. I assured her that if she made the decision to come to a God of mercy, and a place called Mercy, we would pray that God would take care of her child, and that her baby would be born beautiful.

She broke down and began to cry, admitting that she really did not want to get an abortion. Chris made the choice to go to God and to enter the Mercy program to deal with her issues. She was delivered from drugs and gave birth to a beautiful baby boy, who is now a handsome 20-year-old man who stays in touch with me on a regular basis. This young woman who was once so broken is now happily married to a wonderful man and has had the joy of a great relationship with her son all these years. This is a picture of what God's mercy looks like.

The mindset of many people is that someone who has had multiple abortions does not deserve to have a healthy son or to be a happy mom. Many people would say that someone who has been a drug addict does not deserve and could not possibly be equipped to raise a child. But the voice of mercy—the voice of God—says something quite different. Mercy says, *I will meet you where you are and turn your life around.* Mercy says, *I will transform you.* Mercy says, *I will equip you with that which is lacking.* MERCY IS GOD AND GOD IS MERCY. The Bible clearly states in 1 John 4:17 that "as He is, so are we in this world." That means we should be mercy to the people who cross our paths; we are to show them the love of God in tangible ways.

Bottom line, we need to ask God to break our hearts with what breaks His, and to help us to see people the way He sees them—with the eye of faith. We are to speak to people like Chris and tell them that God wants to meet them right where they are. We are to be for them a conduit of mercy—a voice that brings change!

9

HUNGERING
FOR GOD

REBECCA BARLOW
Singer and Guitarist, BarlowGirl

There is a strain of loneliness infecting many Christians,
which only the presence of God can cure.
A. W. TOZER

I believe that life is divided into two types of hungers and desires. The first is a hunger for the things of the physical—our natural desires for food, drink, relationships, and so forth. The second hunger is the hunger for spiritual food—found in the Word and true relationship with the Father, Son and Spirit.

Most of us aren't even aware of our hunger for spiritual sustenance. We feel it groaning in our bodies, but like children we must learn what each hunger is. Until we do, we spend our lives just feeding one hunger and wondering why we feel like we always need more. I have found that it's because we need both to be filled and to feel satisfied. We are here on earth to learn and to grow, but our prize is heaven. Only a moment of our existence is spent here, and yet most of the time, we look to the things of this world to satisfy our deepest longings. We do not even realize when we are hungering for heaven.

I grew up as a lonely child. Even though I was surrounded by a loving family, I can remember thinking I was all alone—that no one understood me. I carried these thoughts with me most of my life. Those feelings were so real and so deep. There was always a lingering loneliness in my heart—one that could not be quenched with family or friendship. I carried this for many years. Loneliness is an interesting phenomenon. It has nothing to do with having people around. You can be in a room full of people and still feel lonely. Loneliness can be felt even in the midst of great relationships, great family or a great marriage. The hunger is there for a reason.

In college, I was at the height of feeling that loneliness; I didn't have any close friends, and no one really knew of my battles. I started college feeling so alone—I felt invisible to everyone. I began to pray for the Lord to help me not feel so lonely. One day during school, He answered my prayer in an odd way. I felt Him tell me, *Look around. Most of these people feel the same way you do.*

This was an awakening moment for me. I had no idea anyone else felt the way I did. When you realize you're not the only one struggling with something, it causes such empowerment and a greater desire to move forward. After all, it's easier to fight on behalf of others than just for yourself. My eyes were opened to how selfishly I had been making my life all about me and my loneliness. I hadn't even looked at the people around me, to see that we had the same struggle. We were all bound to the same chain, and I had no idea.

In that moment, I felt my heart ask, *So, what do you want to do about it?* This revelation launched me into a season during which I would daily ask the Lord to teach me how to reach out and help others not feel lonely. The Lord loves answering this type of prayer. I began to learn how to hear His voice and how to reach out to others. I am an introvert—so while this many not seem like a big deal to you, to me it was challenging and life-changing.

I didn't all of a sudden find myself with numerous friendships that quenched all that loneliness; I didn't get a best friend or a husband out of the deal. I didn't get any of the things that I thought would fill my loneliness. Instead, I learned how to be friends with the Lord. I learned how to talk with Him and obey Him—to do what was uncomfortable. I began realizing how precious my time alone with Him was—so much so that I looked forward to my solitary walks to class and drives to school. I learned how to talk to Him throughout my day. Every time I was by myself, I could spend that time with Him. I was set free from this infectious loneliness; I finally felt like someone knew the depths of me. My victory came in seeing others and putting their needs before my own. In seeing them first, my own need was filled. God loves answering our prayers in ways that not only help us but also help others.

Do I ever feel alone these days? Yes, but when I do, instead of just pondering it and feeling horrible about my life, I take time to talk with the Lord about it. It's amazing how quickly the negative feelings flee when you're with Him. He is always available to us—just waiting for us to take time to talk. He wants to fulfill the loneliness and hunger in all of us.

I foresaw the LORD always before my face,
For He is at my right hand, that I may not be shaken.
Therefore my heart rejoiced, and my tongue was glad;
Moreover my flesh also will rest in hope.
ACTS 2:25-26

10

How Do We Know Who God Is?

DAN KIMBALL
Author and Pastor, Vintage Faith Church,
Santa Cruz, California

*What comes into our minds when we think about God
is the most important thing about us.*

A. W. TOZER

I remember very clearly the first time I read this statement by
A. W. Tozer. At first, I was startled by the incredibly outrageous-
sounding claim it made. But as I processed and thought about it
more, the idea sank into my mind and soul like light permeating
shadows. How incredibly true it was—and how incredibly important it is to understand this in the context of today's culture.

All across the world, many people say the name "God" every
day. But the question is: What do they mean by "God"? That makes
all the difference. I recently listened as a celebrity talked about
God—describing what He is like and what He doesn't like. The
problem was that the way this person described God did not resemble the God of the Bible. The speaker didn't reflect anything
from Scripture as the source of her understanding of God. Rather,
her portrait of God seemed to be based on personal feelings about
what she felt God would be like.

This person described a God who doesn't mind sin, and she in fact shared how "God" even endorses and is glad people participate in some specific sins that were mentioned. The "God" described was also some sort of pluralistic God. Whatever a person chooses to worship, or whatever religious faith one has, it is all the same God, according to this celebrity's definition of God. What one believes about God is important, as those beliefs shape so many other things about us, including what we believe God views as sin. The beliefs about God held by the celebrity I mentioned above have certainly shaped her personal ethics, morals and lifestyle. Where our beliefs about God come from is also incredibly important. Do we base our understanding of God on Scripture, or do we define God using other sources? If people were watching this celebrity explain what she believed God was like, would they then accept the claims of this person and begin using that definition for what they also believe God is like?

Where our definition comes from about who "God" is and what He is like is everything. Our morals, our ethics and our worldviews are all wrapped up in what we believe about God and how we respond to Him and His guidance. How we view ourselves is all wrapped up in what we believe about God and how He views us. As A. W. Tozer stated, what we believe about God does become the most important thing about us.

This truth causes me to respond foremost by wanting to be a serious student of Scripture so I can learn about who God is. Yes, there is some general revelation about God that can be seen in His creation—as we know from Romans 1:20 and Psalm 19:1, which tells us that the heavens declare God's glory and the skies His handiwork. But God communicates so much more about who He is through Scripture.

In the book of Genesis, we learn about God the Creator. We learn about God's love and compassion—and that He is slow to anger—throughout the Hebrew Bible (the Old Testament). We learn about the triune nature of God—His being Father, Son and Spirit—through the Scriptures. In the New Testament, we learn the incredible story of how God became flesh in Jesus and lived amongst us. We learn how Jesus lived a sinless life and became a substitutionary payment for our sin on the cross, and we learn how He was raised from the dead. We learn about the future new heaven and earth God will be creating. All of this shapes my understanding of who God is. So if I believe that what A. W. Tozer says is true, it drives me to a passionate study of God in the Scriptures. I do believe this study needs to be of the whole of the Scriptures. Without a holistic study, we can still define God in ways He is not. If we only look at some sections of Scripture, we could conclude that God is an angry God always looking to smite people. Or if we only look at other sections, we can focus totally on His love and forgiveness, and not on His holiness. Our beliefs about who God is significantly impact how we live. So what we believe about God—what comes into our minds as we think about Him—does become the most important thing about us as we respond in our day-to-day lives in so many ways based on these beliefs.

Another way this truth from A. W. Tozer impacts us is that it should inspire in us a passion to make God known to those who don't know Him. If what we believe about God is the most important thing about us, then we ought to feel an urgency to see as many people as possible know who God is.

I have a specific sense of urgency about the next generation, as I believe we are in a time period when many young people don't know God. They may assume they know God, but it is a God based on their own feelings or on listening to opinions about God that are not necessarily in alignment with what the Scriptures say about Him. We read in Judges 2:10: "After that whole generation had been gathered to their ancestors, another generation grew up who knew neither the LORD nor what he had done" (*TNIV*). So we can see that a generation can arise that does not know God or what He has done throughout history. Their definition of Him becomes one that would not be true or accurate. Again, if what we believe about God is the most important thing about us, then our hearts should break over the idea of future generations not knowing who God is. We must be passionate about doing whatever we can to see future generations know who God truly is.

This short quotation from A. W. Tozer shook my world with a profound and powerful truth. To this day, his words motivate me to be a serious student of Scripture and ignite in me a heart to see others know who God is, since what comes to their minds when they think about God is so important in so many ways. It is in fact the most important thing, as when we know God we learn of His love, grace and holiness—and about His sending His Son, our Savior, to us. If all of this comes to our minds when we think of Him, we respond with awe, worship, repentance and joy, and our entire lives change as we continue to learn who God is. It doesn't end there. As it comes to our minds how God loves people, that knowledge ignites our hearts and gives us the desire to see others know of this incredible, wonderful God.

11

Saying Yes to the Unknown

Lauren Barlow
Drummer and Singer, BarlowGirl

Faith never asks questions when it has been established that God has spoken. Thus faith honors God by counting Him righteous and accepts His testimony against the very evidence of its own senses. That is faith, and of such we can never have too much.

A. W. TOZER

The summer of 1999 is one I will never soon forget. It all started when my mom came to our family during our prayer time and said she felt God had shown her the verse in Luke 5:4 where Jesus says to Peter, "Push out into deep water, and let down your nets for a haul."

That's all He gave her—nothing more. No explanation. Nothing. But somehow she felt that God was asking our family to get ready—to get ready for something big, whatever it may be.

Now, as a 14-year-old, I really had no clue what to expect. Quite frankly, I have never been very partial to fishing, and I wanted nothing to do with that. But, of course, I didn't want to let my dislike of fishing get in the way of something God was trying to say to my family; so, trying to be a good Christian family, we said, "Yes, God, we will get ready for whatever it is You have for us, no matter what."

Saying yes to the unknown with God can be a very scary thing.

What in the world had we just said yes to? We honestly had no clue. But we were a family who always tried to say yes to God, because we knew He was always looking for people who were willing to do anything for Him. We wanted to be those people. Little did we know that less than 12 hours later we would get a phone call that would answer all of our questions from that morning.

My dad received that phone call from a ministry called World Relief. World Relief is a non-profit organization that helps victims of poverty, disease, hunger, war, disasters and persecution. About a month earlier, my dad had called them to ask if there were any way we could get involved with their organization or help in any way. He hadn't heard back from them until now.

The people at World Relief informed my dad that they were involved with helping all the refugees that were coming over to America because of the war happening in Kosovo. Many Kosovars were being sent out of the refugee camps and out of the country because it was too dangerous for them to stay there. I'm sure my dad was wondering where the conversation was going. Then they asked him the big question: "There are 14 Kosovars on a plane to Chicago right now. They aren't supposed to be coming to Chicago, but their flight got messed up so they are stuck. No church will take them because there are too many of them. So, since you recently asked if you could help, do you want to take them in? They will be here first thing in the morning."

My dad asked if he could call them back. He wanted to talk it all over with us first before he committed to doing anything. So he asked my mom what she thought, and of course Mom said without hesitating, "*Yes!* Send them all to us!" Then they asked us kids whether that would be okay, and we all said yes. So Dad called World Relief back five minutes later and told them we would take in all 14 people.

Now, let me share a little background with you. Bottom line, we weren't exactly wealthy. We didn't have some huge house that 14 people could stay in. We lived in a four-bedroom house. Four bedrooms. Fourteen people. (Well, 19 if you count my family and me.) Also, Dad had just quit his job to start a family ministry, so technically we were self-employed. Oh, and did I mention that none of us knew a word of Albanian and they didn't know a word of English? It's true.

If you looked at this situation in the natural, you would have thought we were absolutely crazy. Honestly, when people heard what we were doing, they thought that exact thing. But our family knew that when God calls you to do something, you can never look at it through your natural eyes. If we had tried to figure things out in our heads, we would have just messed up what God was trying to do. Something we all have to know is that God will never call us to do something and forget to walk us through the process. Even though sometimes it feels as though we are walking blindly, we always make it to the end.

If I took the time to share with you every miracle that we saw happen during those two months we had the Behluli family from Kosovo with us, it would fill an entire book. But I will tell you that God provided abundantly more than we would have ever asked for. For two months there was food, clothing, toys, electronics, free doctor visits and free housing for all 14 of them, and anything and everything else we could ever want. Most of it just ended up right on our doorstep.

The family came to us with nothing. Literally, all their bags were lost when they flew here, and they left us with three suitcases each. We could hardly understand each other, but we still spent every waking moment of that summer together. Somehow, there was an understanding.

That was 12 years ago. We haven't seen the Behlulis since they left us. But every time I look back on that summer, I am reminded of God's goodness. And I think of how sad it would have been if we hadn't had the faith to say yes to God. We would have missed out on so much.

That's what faith is all about.

So step out. Go out into the deep and get ready to catch something, even if you aren't that crazy about fishing. Because you never know what amazing things God has for you when you have the faith to simply say yes.

Purity, Then . . .

JOHNNY HUNT
Author, Pastor and Former Southern
Baptist Convention President

No person who has found the blessings of purity and the
joys of the Holy Spirit can ever be defeated.
A. W. TOZER

With each passing year, I become more aware of the great need for personal purity in the inner life of my heart. As David reminded us in Psalm 51, the Lord desires truth in the inward parts. I have often said that when I am sitting on the platform, just as the choir is singing and I am readying myself to preach, nothing means more to me than to know deep in the recesses of my heart that I am a man of personal purity; that, indeed, is a great accelerator to the joy of the Holy Spirit.

When I think of the blessings of purity, James 3:17 comes to mind: "But the wisdom that is from above is first pure, then peaceable, gentle, willing to yield, full of mercy and good fruits, without partiality and without hypocrisy." The Bible teaches that wisdom from above is pure, and the very next word is "then." It is as though the Word is punctuated to remind us that none of the other traits and characteristics of wisdom follow if purity is not in place. Purity serves as the capstone of God's wisdom. When I allow the impurities of this world to flood my soul, I am amazed at how my capacity to be a discerning child of God is diminished; however, when purity is the quality that reigns in my life, I can enjoy the power, joy and confidence that only the Holy Spirit of God can produce in my heart and life. As I strive for purity, its blessings—including the fruit of the Spirit recorded in Galatians 5:22—begin to flow. Not only do I desire purity in my own personal life, but also through the years I have felt the overwhelming responsibility to pass this trait on to my children.

The Lord has blessed me with two beautiful daughters, Deanna and Hollie. They are now grown and have children of their own, but I will never forget the days when God allowed me to speak into their lives and challenge them to be pure, first and foremost for Jesus' sake, and also for the sakes of their future husbands. Both of my girls made the commitment to save themselves for marriage, and they honored that pledge and commitment to Christ and to their father. What a blessing it has been to watch them walk in purity! My favorite Proverb is chapter 20, verse 7: "The righteous man walks in his integrity; his children are blessed after him." My wife's favorite verse comes from John's second epistle; the apostle teaches us that we can have no greater joy than to hear that our children walk in truth (2 John 1:4).

Like wisdom from above, when purity is within—oh, the blessings of God that follow! What a reward for the life of obedience. When I think of purity, I immediately connect the link to joy, deep and abiding peace, genuineness and realness. Purity can not only flow out and touch other lives but also bring a great sense of joy in our own personal life. The newfound life is so overwhelmingly superior to all that one has previously known that there is literally no comparison. As a result, it is no wonder that A. W. Tozer would teach us that this type of life can never be defeated. Who would ever exchange this new life for the life they knew before and left behind?

It has been said that you can teach what you know, but you reproduce who you are. I am grateful that through the years the blessings of purity and the joy of the Holy Spirit have been things I so desire to be resident in my own heart that they might resonate to others around me and serve as an invitation to taste and see that the Lord is good. He chooses to touch others with what He has done in our lives. It is my prayer that the blessings of purity and the joy of the Holy Spirit, which can never be defeated, will be mine both now and for the rest of this life until I see face to face the One who is the epitome of pureness and the overwhelming well of joy.

SIN CANNOT BE HOUSEBROKEN

JONI EARECKSON TADA
Founder and President, Joni and Friends

Holiness is Godlikeness.
A. W. TOZER

Back in college, I had two Christian friends who made it a four-year goal to intentionally reflect Christ to all their fellow students. Professors, too. These young women excelled in reaching out to incoming freshmen, they volunteered at a community food bank, and they led a Bible study in the girls' dorm. They faithfully attended chapel and encouraged others on campus to do the same. They modeled an enthusiastic Christlikeness that won them many admirers. Kind and generous, considerate and caring, these two took their Christianity seriously—at least, on the surface.

My friends, however, had an interesting arrangement. Knowing the warnings that Scripture gives about gossip, they covenanted never to tittle-tattle—except with each other. They didn't have loose tongues with anyone else, because they knew it would be a bad witness (and they were right). But when those two got behind the closed door of their dorm room, did *they* give each other an earful!

My college buddies thought they could control sin and still be like Christ. They minimized and housebroke the sin of gossip in an attempt to make it respectable. Having domesticated this particular sin, they assumed they had tamed it and made themselves masters of it. But now, many years later, those two aren't friends anymore. I suppose Proverbs 16:28 caught up with them: "Gossip separates close friends" (*NIV*). But sin does much more than separate friends. It separates us from God.

My girlfriends wanted so very much to be like Christ in all His compassion and love, but they were only skating on the surface with their deeds and devotion. To be like Christ, first and foremost, is to hate sin. We don't like hearing that. It goes against *everything* in our human nature. We'd much rather emulate the Jesus who looked out for the underdog and welcomed outsiders into His circle. We prefer to model ourselves after Jesus in the way He ministered to the poor and outcast, showcasing what kind and compassionate deeds should look like: touching the leper, blessing the children and healing the sick. These characteristics of Christ resonate with us. We identify. We want to be like that.

But fundamentally, Jesus came to earth to square off against sin. His lifelong goal was to conquer it on the cross, as well as to confront it in the attitudes and actions of people He encountered. So if we want to be like Christ—like God—that means cultivating a disdain for sin—in the world and in our neighborhoods, but mainly in our own hearts.

Tozer was right: Holiness *is* Godlikeness. And Godlikeness is holiness. Yes, God is love, but God is also holy. His holiness is tempered by His love, and His love is perfected by His Holiness. You can't have one without the other. If we truly want to reflect the love of God, we must go on a search-and-destroy mission to uproot every sin, small and great, lurking in our hearts. We must sniff out every hidden fault and snuff out every secret transgression that tries to disguise itself as acceptable. I'm serious about this. Reading A. W. Tozer—who wrote prolifically about eschewing evil—has helped me greatly in my understanding of the necessity of dealing ruthlessly with sin.

I've lived as a quadriplegic in a wheelchair for over four decades, and still, when people ask to pray for my healing, I'll reply, "Would you like to know what I'd really like to be healed of? Walking and running would be great, but I would much rather you pray that I'd quit complaining . . . that I'd be more optimistic and less fearful of the future . . . that I would stop cherishing inflated ideas of my own importance . . . that I'd refrain from keeping a record of my husband's wrongs and always think the best of others . . . that I'd stop hogging the spotlight and give credit to others where it's due. *These* are the areas in which I'd love to be healed!"

Some people might say, "Joni, don't sweat the small stuff. I mean, after all, you *are* paralyzed. Surely God will cut you some slack." But every sin we consider "borderline" gains mastery over us. It does so by deceiving us about its deadly sting. Take the sort of gossip engaged in by my college friends. This indiscretion seems small—rather private, and apparently harmless if done discreetly—but listen to the class in which Romans 1:29-30 puts their habit: "They [those whom God gave over to their own devices] are gossips, slanderers, God-haters, insolent, arrogant and boastful; they invent ways of doing evil" (*NIV*). Yikes! The Lord places gossips and God-haters in the same sentence. I wouldn't call that harmless. Friend, sin is too dangerous to be trained; it cannot be housebroken or domesticated. Ephesians 1:4 is the banner we hold high: "For he chose us in him before the creation of the world to be *holy and blameless* in his sight" (*NIV*, emphasis added).

Oh, I can't wait for the day when I'll truly be holy! It certainly won't happen this side of eternity, but in heaven, our hearts will be made new, pure and fresh. So don't look at my wheelchair and assume I'm looking forward most of all to a new, glorified body; no, I long for a heart completely free of sin. I remember that the core of Christ's plan is to keep rescuing me from sin. Our pain, poverty and broken hearts are not His ultimate focus. He cares about these things, but they are merely symptoms of the real problem. God cares most not about making us comfortable, but about teaching us to hate our transgressions and to grow up spiritually to love Him. His message was: *Sin will kill you, hell is real, God is merciful, His kingdom will change you, and I am your passport.* Whenever people missed this—whenever they started coming to Him to have their pains and problems removed—the Savior backed away.

The Holy Spirit poured out His heart in 1 Peter 1:15-16: "But just as he who called you is holy, so be holy in all you do; for it is written: 'Be holy, because I am holy' " (*NIV*). It's the surest path to Christlikeness. Tozer would agree. So learn a lesson from my two college friends. Think you can tame sin and still be like our Savior? Think again. It'll rip your soul to shreds and separate you from your companions and your God. Friend, aim higher than your transgressions—always aim to be holy, for the pure in heart *will* see God (see Matthew 5:8).

14

GIVING TIME TO GOD

RAVI ZACHARIAS
Apologist, Author and Radio Show Host

I have often wished that there were some way to bring modern Christians into a deeper spiritual life painlessly by short easy lessons; but such wishes are vain. . . . May not the inadequacy of much of our spiritual experience be traced back to our habit of skipping through the corridors of the kingdom like little children through the marketplace, chattering about everything but pausing to learn the true value of nothing?
A. W. TOZER

A. W. Tozer was a unique voice in his time, and the potency of his writing remains timeless. I have read his books repeatedly, and they have always left me yearning for a closer walk with God. The study of God is the highest science, the loftiest pursuit and the mightiest discipline. Its rewards are immeasurable. Tozer's writings express this grand theme with simplicity and sublimity, leaving the reader in hushed silence—for God has been brought near.

I once visited the State Hermitage Museum in St. Petersburg, Russia, with my wife, Margie, and our son. My wife, formally trained as a nurse, is also a student of the fine arts. She studies every little detail, while I do most things in a hurry so we can get them over with and get to our next destination. As we walked through the museum, she examined every painting, while I glanced here and there. I recall its being a magnificent and historic place, but I do not remember much more.

Some years later, I was reading a book by Henri Nouwen, and a story he shared caught my attention. He was teaching at Harvard and had just returned from an exhausting trip of lecturing when he encountered a poster he had never seen before. Two years later, he resigned from his teaching post and went to the State Hermitage Museum to find one painting: the one represented in the poster that he couldn't get out of his mind. It was *The Return of the Prodigal Son*, Rembrandt's depiction of the prodigal son coming home. Nouwen traveled to Russia and sat in front of that painting for three hours—and it changed his life. After this encounter, he knew that he wanted to work with mentally handicapped children and joined a community in Toronto dedicated to this ministry.

Sadly, when I had seen this same painting, I paused for a few fleeting moments and then moved on to the next. I have lived to regret that loss. I went through the museum, as Tozer mused, skipping through the corridors—looking at everything but pausing to learn the true value of nothing.

I remind you how easy it is to do this, even as we are seeking after God. Remember Jesus' disciples in the closing chapter of Luke's Gospel? They are disillusioned, confused and fearful. On the Sunday following Jesus' crucifixion, two of them are walking to a village called Emmaus, about seven miles from Jerusalem. They are talking about everything that happened the previous week, when Jesus Himself appears and walks along with them. But somehow they are kept from recognizing Him. Jesus asks them why they are so downcast, and they respond by asking Him if He is the only visitor to Jerusalem who doesn't know what has happened there over the weekend.

The delightful irony of their question is that *He* is the only one who *does* know what happened! So, Luke tells us, "Beginning with Moses and all the Prophets, he explained to them what was said in all the Scriptures concerning himself" (Luke 24:27, *NIV*).

The seven miles fly by and before they realize it, they arrive in Emmaus. True easterners, the two disciples invite Jesus to join them for dinner. As they sit down to eat, Jesus becomes the host and takes the bread in His hands and blesses it. Suddenly, the disciples are stopped in their tracks, and they recognize Him: *Jesus!* Whether the breaking of the bread reminds them of a meal shared with Him previously or they catch a glimpse of the wounds in His hands, their eyes are opened to Him. Though they spent a couple of hours journeying with Jesus, they did not pause to take in the weight of all that He shared with them until they were seated before Him.

May we sit still long enough to take in what God has for us, for that is the greatest investment we will ever make. As Tozer wisely observes in his chapter "We Must Give Time to God":

> God has not bowed to our nervous haste nor embraced the methods of our machine age. It is well that we accept the hard truth now: the man who would know God must give time to Him! He must count no time wasted which is spent in the cultivation of His acquaintance. He must give himself to meditation and prayer hours on end. So did the saints of old, the glorious company of the apostles, the goodly fellowship of the prophets and the believing members of the holy Church in all generations. And so must we if we would follow in their train!

15

LIVING WITH SACRED EXPECTATION

CYNTHIA HEALD
Author and Navigators Staff Member, Tucson, Arizona

With a sacred expectation, I look for God in ALL
the circumstances of my day.
A. W. TOZER

My friend Virginia and her husband are realtors. At dinner one evening, I asked how the current unfavorable housing market was impacting their lives. Virginia remarked, "Even though this is not a good time to be in real estate, it is an exciting time for us. Each morning we look forward to seeing whom the Lord might bring across our path. We pray for everyone we help and, when possible, we pray with him or her. It's amazing to see the Lord sustain and encourage us—not only physically, but also spiritually."

I don't know if Virginia is familiar with A. W. Tozer's quotation about beginning each day with sacred expectation, but she is someone who beautifully exemplifies this profound thought. Her perspective has challenged and motivated me to continue looking for the Lord in my daily circumstances.

The word "sacred" means holy, sanctified and blessed; and "expectation" means hope, eagerness and excitement. An amplified version of Tozer's reflection might read: "With holy awe and excitement, I look forward to seeing what the Lord has for me this day."

Each morning before getting out of bed, I pray my version of Romans 12:1: "Lord, I present my body to You as a living and holy sacrifice to be used as You please for Your glory." This is my way of committing my day to the Lord, and it also prepares my heart to be aware of His presence. I remember one special time when it was easy for me to see the Lord's hand on my life. I had been seeking God's guidance about whether I should participate in a service project. Still unsure of what to do, I planned to attend the initial meeting and then make a decision. I got into my car, turned the key to start the engine, and immediately discovered that my battery was dead. I recall smiling and praying, as reality set in, "Thank You, Lord, for answering my prayer so specifically, and thank You for Your presence in my circumstances." Eagerly looking for God in all the situations I encounter brings a sense of peace because of the security of His sovereignty. Living with hope for each new day brings a sense of blessing because I am assured of the Lord's love and personal involvement in my life.

How often have you met a friend "by chance" in a public place and discovered something you needed to know or received help in an unexpected way? How often have you acted on the prompting of the Holy Spirit and called someone at just the right time? How often have you seen the Lord's wisdom in shaping your day? I frequently remind myself that the Christian life is the most exciting life there is! Knowing that the Lord directs my steps and uses events in my life to reveal Himself makes every day truly an adventure. I want no other life than one of living in sacred expectation.

In the 1600s, Brother Lawrence was a member of the lay community of the Carmelites in Paris. He served in various menial roles, but he was known for his serene faith and his practice of the presence of God. His words expound and reinforce Tozer's compelling idea of living a life of sacred expectation and continually looking for God in all circumstances:

On a normal working day I would try to fill my waking mind with thoughts of God—in his infinite power, and in his personality. The Bible often began my thinking, and prayer always filled this out and made it personal to me. . . . When I got to the kitchen I would check on the day's menus, assignments, special diets, delivery schedules and so on. Then having got a picture of the day's work, I would briefly but deliberately commit it to God. I often used the same prayer: "O my God, you are always with me. Since I must now, in obedience to your will for me, apply my mind to my day's work, grant me the grace I shall need to continue through it in your presence." . . . Then as the day's routine began, I would know that I was as near God, and he as near me, as if I could have seen him there with my physical eyes.[1]

This is the day the LORD has made. We will rejoice and be glad in it.
PSALM 118:24, *NLT*

Note

1. David Winter, *Closer Than a Brother* (Wheaton, IL: Harold Shaw Publishers, 1971), pp. 158-159.

16

SACRIFICING STYLE AT THE ALTAR OF TRUE WORSHIP

MICHAEL CATT
Pastor, Sherwood Baptist Church, Albany, Georgia

God, Himself, must ever be the object of our worship.
A. W. TOZER

That seems simple enough. It seems obvious at first glance. But the question comes: Is it true in my life personally and in the Church corporately? Sadly, the answer is often no.

To paraphrase Tozer, worship is the missing jewel of the Church today. We've lost the wonder and awe and have often made our praise look weird, lacking power and presence.

As a pastor of a church, I've processed the changing styles of worship over the years. I was saved during the days of the Jesus Movement and have been heavily involved in contemporary Christian music. I have served as an unofficial pastor to a musical group and several individual artists, and I was on the board of another group. On the other hand, I was raised singing the old hymns of the faith. Personally, I like both the traditional hymns and the modern songs of praise. But, then again, worship is not supposed to be about me.

This was the issue for the woman at the well. She wanted to know the location of real worship. Jesus corrected her by reminding her it's not about a place—it's about a Person. (There's nothing like carnal, sinful people talking about worship.)

> Jesus said to her, "Woman, believe Me, an hour is coming when neither in this mountain nor in Jerusalem will you worship the Father. You worship what you do not know; we worship what we know, for salvation is from the Jews. But an hour is coming, and now is, when the true worshipers will worship the Father in spirit and truth; for such people the Father seeks to be His worshipers. God is spirit, and those who worship Him must worship in spirit and truth" (John 4:21-24, *NASB*).

Worship is about Jesus. It's bigger than a day or what happens inside a building. It is a way of life. In reality, we should bring our worship with us to church. Corporate worship should be the overflow of our personal worship.

At the church I pastor, we have made appropriate changes in our worship without changing the focus of worship. We always look at the words and theology of the songs we sing. Just because something sounds good doesn't mean it has sound theology. We did this without having a "worship war." Some did leave the church and did not understand, but my goal was to make sure our worship had life in it.

The key is this: No matter what the style of worship, it must focus on God alone. My preferences do not matter and should not come into account. I should be willing to defer to other styles as long as they are in tune with the essence of true worship. True worship of God causes us to wrestle with a balance that theologians call "the tension between the transcendence and the immanence of God." Worship that makes God the supreme object seeks to balance awe at the holiness of God with the awareness that God is with us.

Why are there worship wars? Because we've made a god of our style preferences. Churches have split, and believers have broken fellowship, over styles. The divide is often not over whether God is worshiped but about what kind of style we prefer.

There are two "gods" being worshiped on any given Sunday: God as He is and God as we've created Him in *our* image. Worship cannot be about catering to the tastes of the congregation or entertaining the saints. Worship, to be true worship, has to maintain God as the focus. The reason our services often lack power is that the god being worshiped is not the one true God. When Isaiah saw the Lord, he didn't raise his hands or jump up and down; he fell on his face.

One missing element in our churches is the "Woe is me" that should come before "Lord, look at how great our worship is." The objective of much of what we find in the twenty-first-century American church is to see if we can get people to react or respond. We are looking for "soulish," emotional worship rather than worship from the heart.

God has called us to worship Him in Spirit *and* truth. Any time there is an attitude that worship is all music and not the Word, God is not the object of worship. "Faith comes by hearing, and hearing by the word of God" (Romans 10:17). A simple study of the Old Testament and Church history would point to the pastor—not the person leading the music—being the worship leader. In the recent worship wars, we've exalted the musician above the Word, the beat above the Bible, and feelings above faith.

Not everything that happens in the house of God is of God. Far too often, we've emphasized intimacy and de-emphasized holiness. God is approachable, but He is still holy. He is meant to be the object of our affections, but even here we don't always get it quite right. My fear is that we have made our feelings and our personal wishes the objects of our affections, and God is an additive, not the source. I'm not sure which offends God more: dead formalism or frenzy.

Just because there is a crowd or you see results, that doesn't necessarily mean God is being worshiped in Spirit and in truth. The Jews crowded into the synagogues, but they rejected God when He showed up in the person of Jesus Christ. Even those who were called "disciples" in the New Testament often turned around and fell away when the stakes were raised. Worship, like discipleship, is not for the bread we receive, but because God is worthy of honor and praise.

What does true worship look like? That's almost impossible to define. However, it would include things like surrender to Christ's lordship, sensitivity to the Spirit, dying to self, and obedience to the Word of God.

I also believe that an altar defines true worship. The altars that Abraham built defined his life. Our lives should be lived at the altar—and true worship of God as He is would alter our lives. We could not sit still in a worship service (no matter what style or form) if we were suddenly struck with the knowledge of whom it is we are worshiping.

Wayne Watson wrote a song a number of years ago that caught my attention with its honest question: "Would I know You?" The lines that stick in my mind are: "Would I know You now if You walked into this place . . . or have the images I've painted so distorted who You are . . . ? I wonder, would I ever know You now?"[1] Would we recognize God if He interrupted our worship routine? Would He recognize us as true worshipers, or would we be revealed as lovers of pleasure and preference?

Note

1. Wayne Watson, "Would I Know You?" from the album *Watercolour Ponies* (Nashville, TN: Word Entertainment LLC, 2007).

17

FREE TO SOAR

BRITT NICOLE
Christian Music Artist

In almost everything that touches our everyday life on earth, God is pleased when we're pleased. He wills that we be as free as birds to soar and sing our maker's praise without anxiety.

A. W. TOZER

This quotation reminds me of who God is and what He desires for my life. Oftentimes I fear that I am not pleasing God. With that fear come anxiety, confusion and worry—all things that are not from God. When I read this statement, it stood out to me that, in almost everything, God is pleased when I am pleased. It was an "oh, yeah" moment for me. God desires that I be happy, just like my earthly father does. In Matthew 7:11, Jesus says, "If you, then, though you are evil, know how to give good gifts to your children, how much more will your Father in heaven give *good gifts* to those who ask him!" (*NIV*, emphasis added). Jesus wants to pour out *good gifts* on us. He came to give us life—and life more abundantly (see John 10:10).

I like the way Tozer put it: "He wills that we be as free as birds to soar and sing our maker's praise." Few of us have experienced this true freedom, and few of us have yet to know what it feels like to soar. When a bird soars, it is no longer moving its wings. There is no more work—no more striving. It is simply riding the wind. When life gets hard, the last thing we feel like we can do is soar and sing, but this is God's desire for us. I feel I could stand to view life a little more like this—less striving, less working and more soaring.

Let's stop trying so hard to please God and instead rest in Him a little more. Let's receive the freedom Christ died for and remember we don't have to be anxious for anything, because God is in control. I love that Tozer ends with just that—the idea of singing God's praise "without anxiety." Ultimately, this is what we were created to do: worship our God and sing His praise. There are times in life when we get so weighed down that we forget how to sing—how to rejoice—but again, this is God's desire for us. He desires that we live such a free, joy-filled life that we can't keep it on the inside. I believe if our hearts are set on worshiping our God and following Him, then we have nothing to be anxious about and nothing to fear. He will shadow and protect us under His wings, and there we can rest without a fear or anxious thought in the world.

WORSHIP: IT'S NOT ABOUT US

NATALIE GRANT
Singer, Songwriter and Four-time
GMA Female Vocalist of the Year

*Worship is no longer worship when it reflects the culture
around us more than the Christ within us.*
A. W. TOZER

The first time I heard this statement, it stopped me dead in my tracks. Maybe that was because it was such a challenging and convicting statement to me personally, but it also sounded so arresting and profound in the context of our modern Christian culture. This definition seems to stand in stark contrast to our common reality in the Church. Most every teaching, book or seminar on the subject will tell you that true worship is a lifestyle—and this is certainly the biblical model (see Colossians 3:23). But we are often challenged to know the difference between this type of worship and the contradictory counterfeits offered up by the church culture nearly everywhere we look. Somewhere between "my entire life as a sacrifice of worship" and "the 30 minutes slotted on Sunday morning for singing praise songs" lives the need for a greater God-shaped consciousness and intentionality.

What does worship actually look like? Just Google that question and one thing is abundantly clear: We live in a fascinating time.

At no other point in history has so much in the way of dialogue, teaching and available resources been amassed and devoted to the subject of worship. But it's also true that the massive marketplace of ideas has not made the subject clearer or easier. Quite the contrary: It's virtually impossible to understand how deeply we are imprinted by our culture in our approach to our faith and the worship of our God. The truth is, the incredible corporate worship expression of our modern Church age is marked by one of the greatest challenges that faces the Church at large in this era of history: consumerism.

We carry on, at times, like all of this is actually for us: Does a church engage in "our style" of worship? Even the more seemingly noble question, "Am I ministered to?" in the end makes us unwitting participants in the narcissistic consumer culture that seeks to divert us from the very reason we exist—the true worship and adoration of God—and tries to make us believe that worship exists for something we can derive out of it.

One thing is sure: For all the things that worship is not, it is the accurate mirror. Designed by God as our ultimate life activity and purpose, it can simultaneously reflect our Creator and also illuminate our heart's position towards Him. The fundamental biblical truth is that worship was not created for us; we were created for it— for the singular pleasure of almighty God.

As a recording artist who sings Christian music, I often fall into the trap of thinking that what I do on stage is my ultimate act of worship. I am, after all, singing songs about Jesus. How easy it is for me to display my acts of worship, leading others to believe I have a worshiper's heart. While I pray that, more often than not, my career and music ministry are offered from a pure place of lifting high the name of Jesus, my concern about success can get in my way.

So I am compelled to ask this question: What does my worship say about me—or rather, about my great God? I pray you will ask yourself this same question. The greatest form of worship comes through living an authentic life of humility, service and love. As we seek to let our lives be marked by these things, we will reflect the Christ we claim to serve. When this happens, worship will not be what we do. It will be what we live.

19

A BEAUTIFUL SURPRISE

DARLENE ZSCHECH
Singer, Songwriter and Pastor

*The yearning to know what cannot be known, to comprehend the incom-
prehensible, to touch and taste the unapproachable, arises from the image
of God in the nature of man. Deep calleth unto deep, and though polluted
and landlocked by the mighty disaster theologians call the Fall, the soul
senses its origin and longs to return to its source.*

A. W. TOZER

This magnificent statement by Tozer is one of the reasons that his
life was so celebrated, as his thought processes and arguments for
the truth of Christ have for generations challenged those of us in
the Church to pursue authenticity in all we do. It is to this end
that we hear his heart describe the value of wholehearted worship
and our constant pursuit of being near to the only One who completely satisfies.

One of the beautiful surprises about the worship of God is
that when we truly encounter His presence, that sense of being
home is so very real as our spirit resonates in its place of origin—and
longs for more. This is the beauty of the Lord in our lives: His
majesty, grace and power being revealed in us, healing us and gently making us whole.

Personally, I know in my heart of hearts that this reality of His strength in my weakness, His life in my soul, is the reason why I am devoted to His worship and worth-ship. The longing in the core of who I am only finds the depth of satisfaction that it craves when I am in prayer and, on purpose, found in adoration. This is why my heart leaps at Tozer's statement.

James 4:8 says it simply: "Come near to God and he will come near to you." So let's make the pursuit of more of Jesus in our lives the main thing. With His will as our goal, and His light shining in us and through us, I truly pray that we will live as His felt expression across the earth, beautifully graced with understanding and resolve, standing resplendent in His image and living defined by His presence.

20

FASCINATED

> ## BRITT MERRICK
> Pastor, Reality Santa Barbara, California

We are called to an everlasting preoccupation with God.
A. W. TOZER

We are a culture of fascination. Every modern gadget given to us has allowed us to be further fascinated with all sorts of amazing things. In an instant, we can view Google images of deep space and minute cellular structure alike—things no previous generation has ever seen. We also have more entertainment and money than the world has ever before known. The possibilities seem endless, and we are fascinated.

Fascination has become preoccupation. We aren't just excited about these things—they consume us. We're obsessed. Yet, strangely, the more we indulge in them, the less they seem to satisfy us. Economists, in their context, call this phenomenon the law of diminishing returns. Addicts call it: "I need more to get the same feeling." Most of us call it: "I want the latest version. I need the iPhone 5!" We are seldom satisfied.

The psalmist lived in a different reality. He could say to the Lord, "You have given me greater joy than those who have abundant harvests of grain and new wine" (Psalm 4:7, *NLT*). Again he would sing, "Your unfailing love is better than life itself" (Psalm 63:3, *NLT*). He had discovered that there is nothing in this world that satisfies like God and His love—that, in a life spent in fascination with God, there are no diminishing returns.

The truth is that we were made to glorify God and enjoy Him forever.[1] Nothing less than that will do. Augustine would say, "My soul is restless until it rests in you, O God." But we are preoccupied with many other things, and so our restlessness persists.

All the while, there is a nagging utterance within the Christian that whispers, "God is better. He is your rest and joy." This is the Spirit, calling us to an everlasting preoccupation with God. He entreats us to be captivated, charmed and entranced—fascinated—with who God is.

But how can we see past the enticing items and activities that vie for our fascination in the push and pull of everyday life?

Perhaps realizing that we, in fact, are God's preoccupation will help us—thinking deeply on the truth that we are His beloved, His obsession. He loves us with an everlasting love. He calls us His special possession. He has inscribed us on His palms. His love caused the Son to drape Himself in, and be crucified by, humanity in order to save God's objects of affection—us! In Christ, God has lavished His love on us and means to treat us with unending kindness now and forever.

It's not that we are, or ever were, deserving of such love and kindness. We are not. It is, rather, that in God's infinite kindness and love, which spring from His very essence and nature, He has done the unthinkable—loved most those who deserved least. He does not love us because we are valuable; rather, we are valuable because He loves us.

Since we were never good, but only loved, we are free from ever having to try to be good. Instead, we are called to be preoccupied—fascinated—with the Lover. When our fascination—more rightly, our love—is directed toward the Lover, we are finally free. Free from a sense of failure and unwantedness. Free from running in circles, trying to prove that we are worthy or lovable. Free from restless, anxious, lustful, angry and wrong preoccupations. We are finally free from living a life of perpetual dissatisfaction. In being loved by the Lover and loving Him back, we are at rest. We are living the life we were meant to live.

The gadgets will still clamor for our attention, but we have a deeper call—one that reminds us of a truer, better fascination. One that brings us back to the fact that we are, and always have been, made for and called to an everlasting preoccupation with God and enjoyment of Him forever.

The first thing by Tozer I ever read was the closing prayer from the first chapter of *The Pursuit of God*. In my memory, it went something like: "God, I have tasted Thee and it has both satisfied me and made me thirsty for more." That changed my life. I've been in pursuit of God ever since.

May I now suggest you pray this with me: "God, show me the way of life, granting me the joy of Your presence and the pleasure of living with You forever."[2]

Notes

1. *The Westminster Larger Catechism*, Question One.
2. Adapted from Psalm 16:11, *NLT.*

21

LIVING FROM
THE LIFE WITHIN

KENN GULLIKSEN
Founding Pastor, Vineyard Christian Fellowship

It is God who works in and through us, if only
we would let God do His work.
A. W. TOZER

On a blustery day several years ago, my wife, Joanie, and I were walking around Balboa Island, California. We stopped by the sea wall as we watched a couple of young boys struggling to row a small dinghy up the bay. They were rowing against the wind and tide, and they soon beached the little boat, exhausted. As Joanie and I were about to walk on, we saw another couple of boys appear, this time in a small sailboat. Although the wind and tide were equally against them, they were not just making progress but were relaxed, laughing, and enjoying the journey. They simply knew how to sail; how to rest from their own struggling and cooperate with the "inspiration" of the wind.

Aiden Wilson Tozer received inspiration, revelation, about ceasing from his own labor, resting in His intimacy with Jesus, and continually allowing the Holy Spirit in him to will (desire) and work (serve with power) through him. Tozer inspires us because he invites us into that same essential truth: the source, the origin, of all we are and do must be the breath of God, the Holy Spirit in us. We all know intuitively when a book, a message, was written by a human soul rowing or by the Holy Spirit sailing. We're told in 2 Timothy 3:16, "All scripture is given by inspiration of God" (*KJV*). The *New International Version* has it, "All Scripture is God-breathed." The Greek word for inspiration is a combination of *theos* ("God") and *pneo* ("to breathe"). Genuine inspiration is the result of "a divine influence directly exerted upon the soul." We are inspired when the source—the origin—of a book or a message is the Holy Spirit, not human soulishness. By the same token, we inspire others when the source of our words and actions is the Holy Spirit, not our human soulishness.

I was greatly helped in understanding this when I read these words from an inspiring teacher: "The soul (emotions, intellect and will) must come to the Cross daily, *not to be destroyed, but to give up its right to rule.*" The light came on for me as I saw that the kingdom of God is the rule and reign of the Holy Spirit over my soul—over my emotions, feelings and desires—and over my very thinking ("bringing every thought into captivity to the obedience of Christ" [2 Corinthians 10:5]). The Holy Spirit used A. W. Tozer to inspire me—to speak to my spirit the things of the Spirit—and that inspiration has been life-changing.

Near the beginning of our pastoral ministry, Chuck Smith of Calvary Chapel (in Costa Mesa, California) blessed my wife, Joanie, and me to "plant" a church the Holy Spirit had conceived in our hearts. The Inspirer had spoken to us to go to west Los Angeles. The Lord first sent us to El Paso, Texas, for a year to help with a church plant there, and then He brought us back to Costa Mesa for a year because my heart was not right in a relationship, and it needed to be before moving ahead. This was during the height of the Jesus Movement, and all I really knew was that I loved Jesus with all my heart and wanted to obey His leading. As our new congregation began meeting, I sat on a stool, led worship with the three chords I knew on the guitar, taught the Bible verse by verse (as well as I could), and invited people to follow Jesus, to be baptized, and to be filled with the Holy Spirit.

During these early years of ministry, I was greatly inspired by two men: A. W. Tozer and a dear old English missionary friend named Norman Grubb. Tozer's writings inspired me particularly in their emphasis of intimacy with Jesus over "religion," and Norman personally taught me about vine/branch union—Christ in me. The central truth was that I was to love the Lord with all my heart and to serve others from the overflow of that intimacy.

The Holy Spirit very clearly told me to name our fledgling congregation "The Vineyard Christian Fellowship." It was 1974. We quickly grew as the Lord brought into our midst the unemployed, the rich, the homeless, rock stars, sports stars, celebrities, celebrity wanna-bes, young, old, and every combination of colors you could imagine. Three hundred members of our church family were Jews who decided to follow Jesus. It was all the work of the Holy Spirit. Our hearts were open, hungry and filled with joy! We gathered and sang "Immanuel," "The Hiding Place" and other harmonious songs of worship. Unbelievers wept as they walked in the door during worship. We planted a dozen other Vineyards around the country—not by being deliberate, but more in the way of unplanned pregnancies. People who had been with us went out and started groups that became churches based on our model.

After eight years or so, the still, small voice of the Inspirer became harder for me to hear. I began to work in my own strength and quickly grew weary in well-doing. I lost my joy, because the joy of the Lord is our strength. I started trying to prove to God that I was worth saving. Ministry (service) turned into exhausting work.

In my despair, I remembered Tozer. I remembered Norman Grubb. I remembered the Holy Spirit. The Inspirer brought me to Philippians 2:12-13 (from which Tozer draws in the quotation at the beginning of this chapter): "Continue to work out your salvation with fear and trembling, for it is God who works in you to will and to act according to his good purpose" (NIV). After having begun in the Spirit, I had gotten lost in success. I was working all right, but working in my own strength to try to get what I already had—God's unconditional love and acceptance—and what I thought I needed—validation from people.

The point of the verse is: *It is God who works in you to will and to act.* The Holy Spirit is in me; He's my life, and He's seeking to rule and reign over my soul. It is He who gives me "will"—or supernatural desire. It is He who enables me to "act"—or to serve in supernatural power. He is the origin of all God is and does in me. It's basically like the difference between rowing and sailing. The rower struggles to get wherever he needs to go, while the sailor uses the enablement of wind.

Dear friend, if you've started well but gotten stuck in self-effort—in seeking approval through performance and trying to prove to God that you were worth saving—may these words from the Inspirer inspire you. May God breathe life into you as you live from the Holy Spirit in you. May you once again fall in love with Jesus so fully that you find rest in His finished work and allow His Spirit to give you the desire and the power to finish your work well, to His glory.

I'm reminded of a song I wrote 40 years ago, as the Inspirer was first revealing my lover, Jesus, in me:

I met you there in the dawning of morning, the secret and tender time that we share together;
 You touched my heart, we communed in the first light of day in a way that showed you really care,
  You care for me!
 You whispered words of encouragement, love, joy and peace, words of life to my emptiness;
 You smiled and conquered my heart with affection that overcame all my fears, all my loneliness,
  You care for me!
 And in that moment of time, so sublime, your still, small voice tenderly spoke;
 I couldn't help but commit all my life, all my love to your trust and know
  That never again could I in my pride ever let your love be denied,
   For you are my life, you are my love, you are my hope!

Father, we quiet our souls and thank You that You live in us by Your Spirit. We thank You that You are life, love, joy, peace and power. All that we will ever need has already been given! Forgive us for begging You to give us what we already have. Rule and reign over our souls, Holy Spirit, and fulfill every purpose and intent You have for each of us as we celebrate Your life and live from the life within, in Jesus' name.

GOD IN THE DARK

JAMIE OWENS COLLINS
Songwriter, Worship Leader and Recording Artist

True faith rests upon the character of God.
A. W. TOZER

I am a child of the Jesus Movement. During my teenage years, God revealed Himself to my spiritually hungry generation in a fresh, almost palpable way. Whether we met for Bible study or to sing praises at a beach baptism, we were captivated by a strong sense of God's presence. Music was our language of thanks and praise as we saw lives miraculously changed by the power of God. Our faith soared.

Joined by friends such as Barry McGuire, Larry Norman, Keith Green and the Second Chapter of Acts, I dedicated my music to God's service. By the time I was 19, I had two solo albums under my belt and had traveled extensively throughout the United States, Europe and Australasia, often alone. I sang in churches, schools, prisons, coffee houses and arenas, and I made TV and radio appearances. It never occurred to me to be afraid. God was with me. I was a girl on a mission—full of faith and expecting God to do amazing works.

As an intrepid 20-year-old, I married record producer Dan Collins. Without skipping a beat, I recorded a couple more albums, added kids—one, two, three—to the luggage and kept going, singing and speaking in many parts of the world. There wasn't much time for details like eating and sleeping. It was all right though, because Philippians 4:13 said that I could "do all things through Him who strengthens me" (*NASB*). Besides, why else did God make coffee, right?

As my public ministry grew, I began to ask God to teach me more about faith. I probably should have been more specific. I wanted a powerful faith that would result in miraculous answers to prayer. Wouldn't it be wonderful to lay hands on the sick and watch them recover, to see instant intervention in impossible circumstances, to pray with authority and watch things happen? But God has His own way of answering prayer. Within months of asking Him to strengthen my faith, I was plunged into my own "dark night of the soul."

As Dan and I prepared for the next European tour, I began experiencing a terrible sense of dread, as if something awful were about to happen. Soon I started having strange, debilitating physical symptoms. These "attacks" occurred frequently, with intense sensations sometimes lasting for hours. During an attack, I couldn't concentrate or sleep—often I couldn't even stand up. I prayed, quoted Scripture, rebuked the devil—I tried every sure-fire thing I'd been taught to do when the enemy attacks. Nothing worked! I was devastatingly disappointed and confused. We canceled the tour and all the engagements I had booked.

Over the next four years, the attacks became more frequent. When I *was* able to function, I felt as though the sky would fall at any minute—even on beautiful, sunny days. I had lived my whole life with a sense of God's presence and taken it for granted. Now, for the first time, I had lost that sense. I was having my first real encounter with doubt. *Where is God in all this?* I thought. *Is He really good and kind and loving? Did Jesus really mean it when He said, "I will never leave you or forsake you?"* I wondered if I'd built my whole life on an imaginary friend.

I picked up a book called *The Thomas Factor*, written by my dear friend Winkie Pratney, a brilliant "mad scientist" and Bible scholar from New Zealand. Winkie's insights on doubt gripped my attention: "Doubt is not the opposite of faith. . . . You can trust God in the middle of doubt just as you can be brave in the midst of fear. You come down on the side of what God says and you go on anyway."[1] That's when I realized I had a decision to make. Even though I couldn't sense that God was anywhere in my vicinity, I had to choose to trust that He was who He claimed to be—that He was right in the middle of this battle with me and up to something good. Although my life had taken a turn I'd never expected, I finally saw that my faith could truly rest on the character of my loving God—and on nothing else. I chose to believe He truly loved me. I decided to put all my trust in God's character and, as best I could, walk by faith. Hmmm . . . FAITH. Isn't that where I had started?

Once I determined to take God at His word, I began to offer a "sacrifice of praise," playing and singing along with worship music even though I was still suffering—and the road to healing began.

At the ongoing encouragement of friends and family who had been praying for me, I visited my doctor. He surprised me with a diagnosis of clinical depression and anxiety disorder. I, of course, had never considered that this might be my problem. Christians didn't get depressed or anxious, right? I knew nothing of the physicality of these debilitating disorders; I had always assumed they were somehow moral or spiritual failures. Boy, did I learn some humility and compassion! The truth was that I had so foolishly worn myself down with a Wonder Woman lifestyle—all in the name of "ministry"—that my adrenal system had just fried. In my youthful zeal, I thought I was stepping out in "faith" by presumptuously trying to do "all things." I gained a new understanding of Philippians 4:13: I can do all things—the things that *God* gives me to do—through Him who strengthens me. God has no limits—but I do. Once I got some medical help and started making wiser lifestyle choices, I was back to health and peace in a couple of months.

Dr. Tozer was right: "True faith rests upon the character of God." Looking back, I can see that God did answer my prayers. He did teach me about faith—just differently than I'd expected. I learned that faith isn't about getting prayer answered the way we want. It's not about believing hard enough or praying with just the right words, and it's not about doing "ministry" until we drop. Faith is about a relationship with Someone who is trustworthy, even when He doesn't explain Himself. Sometimes faith is a decision we make that flies in the face of our emotions or what we can see. Faith is based solely on the proven character of our loving but unfathomable Father God.

Are you walking through the darkness of disappointment and discouragement right now? Have your expectations been dashed? Do you wonder if you have fallen off of God's radar? Isaiah 50:10 says, "Who among you fears the LORD? Who obeys the voice of His Servant? Who walks in darkness and has no light? Let him trust in the name of the LORD and rely upon his God." Yes, even a godly person can walk through the dark for a season. But I love Psalm 139:12: "The darkness and the light are both alike to You." God can see in the dark! He is in that dark place with you. Nothing frightens Him or takes Him by surprise. And He loves you. He will not break His promise that He'll never leave or forsake you—even when life gets rough. That is just not His way. He is up to something good, and He will bring you into the light again. Let your faith rest on the faithful character of God.

Call me crazy, but I'm still asking God to teach me about faith. I still long to see the miraculous, but I now understand that real faith will always hinge on trusting God's character. A friend recently told me, "Faith isn't faith until it's been tested. Before that, it's just belief." I have come to understand that every test of our faith is also a test of God's faithfulness—and He never fails a test!

Note

1. Winkie Pratney, *The Thomas Factor* (Old Tappan, NJ: Chosen Books, 1982).

23

THOUGH I'M UNWORTHY

LISA ROBSON
Information Technology/Worship VJ

God loves you not because you are worthy, but because He is God and you are a fixture in His mind.

A. W. TOZER

There was a time in my life when I felt that God couldn't love me, because I was so unworthy. I had hurt someone close to me and ruined a friendship. More than that, I knew that when I hurt that person, I hurt God—so there was no way God could love me now. I couldn't even love myself.

It was a dark time. I was tormented day in and day out by the thought that I had messed up so bad that God couldn't love me. During this season, I believed every single lie that Satan told me, mostly variations on the theme: *How could God love someone who would do something that would hurt someone else—and their best friend, at that?* This went on for about six months, until one day I had an especially bad day at work. I had gotten an email that said, "Bad things are always going to follow you," and I began to yell out to God, saying, "I knew You couldn't love me, because I messed up, and there's nothing I can do to change what I did."

I got in the car and began to drive to Starbucks. While I was driving, all I could hear was: *Don't you see you'll never be anything—*

that not a person loves you, and bad things are always going to follow you
around? You should just end it now. You have a gun. Just pull it out, be-
cause no one is even going to care you're gone. I went through the Starbucks drive-thru, ordered my drink, pulled into the parking lot
and sat there.

I didn't think I could take much more. So, as I drank my coffee, I opened up my console and pulled out my gun. I set the coffee down and placed the gun to my head. I yelled at God, saying,
"I guess this is it; I have someone who hates me, and most of all I
know You do, too." I pulled the trigger . . . and the gun just clicked.

In that moment, I sensed God asking me, *How many times have*
I told you I loved you? The memories rushed back. There was a lady
at a conference who came up to me and hugged me and said, "God
said to tell you He loves you." Then again, a month later, I was at
church; an usher walked up to me and said, "God told me to tell
you He loves you." I remember shaking my head and thinking,
How? How can You love me? His response: *I love you no matter what you*
have done. I love you, and it doesn't matter if anyone else in the world loves
you or not.

He loves me so much that He wouldn't let me hurt myself. He
reminded me that He wouldn't have sent His Son to be beaten beyond recognition for someone He didn't treasure. He showed me
that I was worth something—that I was valuable to Him. He loved
me so much that He sent Jesus to pay for that mistake—for that
mess-up I thought was so awful it would make Him hate me.

In that moment, my heart began to heal. It didn't happen over-
night; it was a day-to-day process. I had to forgive myself—to let
go of all my hurt and the things I couldn't change—as I began to
move forward. It has been a hard road to finally get to a place
where I can say I've let it go, and I can look back at what happened
and see what I came out of through God's grace and mercy. Yes, it's
been hard, but I can now walk in freedom, knowing I am loved by
the King.

No matter how much you or I have messed up—no matter the
sin—He loves us. We are just like the lady who was brought before
Jesus—the one who had committed adultery. All the people were

trying to see what He would say, since the rule was to stone any person caught in adultery. Instead of condemning her for her sin, Jesus reached down and started drawing in the sand. It was almost like He was saying, "I'm not afraid to get dirty to save you. I'll reach down and clean your mess however many times it takes to show you that I love you, and that I want you in eternity with Me." I love the part when He says the person among the crowd who had no sin should cast the first stone—and one by one they left. You see, no matter what, He will forgive you and love you, because He wants you. People may not forgive you or love you, but the GOD who created the universe cares for you and loves you more than you or I will ever deserve. Not because we are worthy, but just because He does.

24

EMBRACE GRACE

JUDAH SMITH

Lead Pastor, The City Church, Seattle, Washington

God expects of us only what He Himself has supplied.
A. W. TOZER

Ever tried to hug someone who doesn't know how to hug back? You go for a warm bear hug, and you're met with a one-armed, lead-with-the-hip side hug—if you're lucky, you might also get a pat on the back and a mumbled, "Love ya too, bro." It's awkward, like hugging a mannequin.

That's how Christians often react when grace comes at them. God tries to smother us with a great big grace embrace, but we don't know how to hug back. So we stand there, stiff and uncomfortable, waiting for it to be over so we can go back to our task of trying to deserve His love.

Remember the parable of the prodigal son (see Luke 15:11-32)? After wasting his father's possessions, and nearly dead with hunger, the boy musters the courage to return home and beg to become a servant in his father's household. That's the best he can hope for; it's all he deserves.

But while he is still a long way off, his father sees him, runs to meet him and embraces him. Talk about awkward. In those days, fathers didn't run or express that kind of emotion in public—especially to a son who had dishonored the family.

The son—just like the legalistic audience listening to Jesus—doesn't know how to respond to his father's lavish display of affection. He tries to give his rehearsed speech—to convince his father to receive him based on merit.

But his father just laughs and cuts him off, then throws a party for him. This loving father doesn't care about merit; he cares about his son.

That's grace. It's surprising, overwhelming and so good it's uncomfortable.

Most of us don't have trouble believing that God could save us by grace. We know we were sinners, and that Jesus died for us—that He loved us first.

So how did we come up with the idea that as Christians we now have to earn everything? Why do we worry that God is impatient with our failings, that He won't use us if we mess up, or that we have to accomplish amazing feats to impress Him?

Christianity is way more about God than about us. We love because He first loved us. He is the initiator; we are the responders. He gave to us; therefore we give back.

Grace can't be a backup plan in case our good works fail. Grace is the foundation of our good works. Sure, Paul tells us in Philippians to "work out your own salvation with fear and trembling." But it's the next phrase that makes this command possible: "For it is God who works in you both to will and to do for His good pleasure" (Philippians 2:12-13).

Pride is one of the greatest enemies of grace. We want to be good enough; we want to earn everything—that appeals to our egos. But we need to learn how to receive so that we will be able to give back out of the abundance of what God has given us.

Of course God expects great things from us. But like any loving father, His definition of "great" is somewhat relative.

My four-year-old son, Zion, plays soccer. Actually, that's overstating it. He runs around a field with a bunch of other four-year-olds, and once in a while someone accidentally bumps into the ball.

The other day I was at practice—not a game, just practice—and the ball squirted out of the pack and towards the opposing goal. Then I saw Zion break out of the herd, chasing the ball, and something came over me.

Now, soccer practice for four-year-olds is essentially a cheap substitute for daycare, so I was the only parent on the sidelines. But when Zion had a chance to score a goal, you would have thought it was the World Cup of preschoolers.

I ran down the sidelines, screaming, "Kick the ball, Zion, kick the ball!" The coach probably thought I needed therapy, but I didn't care. This was my son, and he was awesome.

Then, a miracle: He kicked the ball, and it bounced off his ankle and into the goal. Next thing he knew, I was swooping him up onto my shoulders, parading him around the field and proclaiming how great he was.

And I was sincere.

Some of us are way too "emo"—too up and down. *I sinned, and God's mad at me.* Ever heard of the foreknowledge of God? He knows—and has always known—about our future failures. If He loves us now, knowing what we'll do wrong tomorrow, why are we doubting? If He loved us last week, He loves us this week, too. Repent, receive it and move on!

Grace is a term we throw around a lot but hardly understand, much less know what to do with. It's like a gift your aunt bought you—and then she stands there while you open it. You don't have any idea what it is, but she's asking if you like it. "Yes! Totally! Exactly what I wanted." Then you put it in the closet, because you don't know what else to do with it.

My all-time favorite definition of grace is this: "God meeting us at our point of need in the Person of Jesus Christ."[1] John 1:16, speaking of Jesus, states, "And of His fullness we have all received, and grace for grace." Grace isn't an abstract, impersonal doctrine. It isn't a tendency of God. It's a Person: Jesus.

If grace is a concept, we can ignore it or take advantage of it. But when we realize that it's a Person, our whole perspective changes.

My wife, Chelsea, loves me with all her heart. She puts up with my quirks and failures. She's been faithful to me for 11 years and counting. Never once in our marriage has her amazing love caused me to think, *Hey, maybe I'll cheat on her once or twice. She'll still love me. I can hurt her and then come back to her—it's all good.*

When we look into the eyes of grace and embrace grace—when we see Him and feel His relentless love—we aren't motivated toward sin but toward righteousness.

It's time to stop struggling in the arms of forgiveness, to stop making lame excuses and impossible promises, to stop striving to prove something to a God who already knows the truth about us.

Just embrace grace.

Note
1. Jack Hayford, *New Spirit-Filled Life Bible* (Nashville, TN: Thomas Nelson, 2002), notes on John 1:16.

25

DISCOVERING THE KNOWABLE GOD

TOMMY WALKER
Worship Leader/Musician

For now begins the glorious pursuit, the heart's happy exploration of the infinite riches of the Godhead.
A. W. TOZER

Many years ago, I was house sitting an abandoned house for my brother, who was a real estate agent. I had just returned from a missions trip and found myself in a very low and discouraged state. For several years before this time, I had been in Christian bands—serving the Lord the best I knew how—but my relationship with God had grown dry, and I felt a real lack of direction for the first time in my life. It was at this point that someone told me to read *The Pursuit of God* by A. W. Tozer.

I remember coming back to that empty, quiet house each night and slowly working my way through the book. It was as if I was being told for the first time: You can really know this God you have been serving all these years! Two words that always hit me when I read Tozer are "longing" and "wander." Those nights I spent alone reading *The Pursuit of God* for the first time were no exception.

At the end of each of the 10 chapters in the book there is a prayer. I remember kneeling and praying those prayers of longing and pursuit. I read them with great reverence and awe. The presence of God became so strong that I literally kept looking around the room to see who was there. We make this claim way too often, but in this case it is true: This was truly a life-changing experience! Writing about it rekindles the fire in me even now. Thank You, Lord!

Before this experience, I was what you might call a typical Christian. Like so many, I was trying to serve God and be made into His image, but it hadn't really crossed my mind to personally and intimately pursue knowing Him.

"Now this is eternal life: that they may know you, the only true God, and Jesus Christ, whom you have sent" (John 17:3, *NIV*). This verse, which Tozer quotes in his book, brings me to the point of this testimonial. God—while He is mysterious, invisible and beyond anything our minds could ever comprehend—is knowable. He is the most relational being in the universe and is ever waiting to reveal Himself to us! If God were merely an idea out there in the cosmos—or just a set of rules for us to follow—there would be no reason to truly long for Him and want to know Him. Yet He said the greatest commandment of all is to love Him!

God used A. W. Tozer to turn a directionless, dry Christ-follower into a joy-filled, passionate worshiper, and this is why I am a worship leader to this day! God's anointing in Tozer's writings has played a huge role in giving me this great passion to make people *long for God, worship God and, out of that, serve God!* I am always grateful for a chance to share my story and hopefully inspire someone else to take one step closer to the infinite riches of knowing our precious Lord!

26

HEAVEN'S JOY

DUDLEY RUTHERFORD
Senior Pastor, Shepherd of the Hills Church,
Porter Ranch, California

*God is going to be as pleased to have you with Him in
heaven as you will be to be there with Him.*
A. W. TOZER

Count me as one of the many who are eagerly awaiting the journey
to a place called heaven. What a day that will be when we get to
see our loved ones who have died, exit the struggles and pains of
this life, and experience the place so intriguingly described in Revelation 21:1-27. This vivid passage of Scripture tells us that the city
of heaven will have streets made of pure gold, walls decorated with
every kind of precious stone (such as sapphires and rubies), and
12 gates made of a single pearl each. There will be no sun or moon,
because heaven will be illuminated by the glory of God. Death and
darkness will never enter this majestic kingdom, and there will be
no more sin, sorrow or sickness. Can you imagine?

Hollywood imagery would lead you to believe that you will be
sitting on a cloud in heaven, strumming a harp all day. But in ac-
tuality, it's going to be a boisterous wedding feast (see Matthew
22:2 and 25:10)—a celebration like no other—and you are going to

enjoy yourself! Of course, the ultimate prize is that Jesus will be there. That's what I'm looking forward to the most. Each of us, as believers, will be with Christ our Lord for all of eternity, and we will *never ever* have to say goodbye.

As you look forward to this grand and glorious reunion, it is important to fully absorb what Tozer aptly noted in his surprising statement: God will be just as excited to see you as you will be to see Him—if not more so! But how do we know this?

First, we know it because of the sheer detail that He has put into creating heaven. As a mother bird lovingly and meticulously builds a nest in preparation for the impending arrival of her babies—but in an exponentially greater way—God has been putting the finishing touches on your eternal home. Shortly before His crucifixion, Jesus revealed that He soon would go to His Father's house "to prepare a place for you" (John 14:2). If the Lord created the splendor of our universe in a mere six days, can you imagine how awesome heaven will be when He has spent the last 2,000 years on its magnificent construction?

Second, we know this because of the depth of God's love. Did you know that He loves you as much as He loves Jesus? That may be shocking, but it's true! According to John 17:23, when praying to God about His earnest desire for unity among all believers, Jesus Himself made this request: "Let the world know that you sent me and have loved them *even as you have loved me*" (*NIV*, emphasis added).

Since God gave up His one and only Son (see John 3:16), it's fair to say He spared no expense in order to get you to heaven. I am reminded of the story of the man who took his son and his son's friend sailing off the Pacific Coast. Though the man was an experienced sailor, he could not foresee a fast-approaching storm that soon pounded their boat with furious waves, causing it to capsize. The three were swept into the ocean. Grabbing a rescue line, the father had to make the most agonizing decision of his life: to which boy he would throw the other end of the lifeline. He had only a few seconds in which to choose. Knowing that his son was a Christian, and that his son's friend was not, the father yelled out, "I love you, son!" and threw the lifeline to his son's friend. By the time the father had pulled the friend back to the capsized boat, his son had disappeared beneath the raging swells.

Romans 5:8 declares, "But God demonstrates his own love for us in this: While we were still sinners, Christ died for us" (*NIV*). God's love for you is unfathomably sacrificial. It can be measured by the dimensions of an old rugged cross at Calvary, upon which Jesus shed His blood for your sins and mine. He loves you, and He wants to spend eternity with you.

When God created Adam and Eve, as chronicled in Genesis 2, He provided everything for them so that they might live in a peaceful paradise and enjoy walking with Him daily. Though they broke that perfect fellowship with their Creator through sin and disobedience, God desired to restore that which was broken and to once again have an intimate and eternal relationship with His children.

Through the death, burial and resurrection of Jesus Christ, our heavenly Father has provided a way for you and me to be reconciled with Him. If you haven't yet put your faith and trust in Jesus, please commit today to follow Him and serve Him. God, like the father of the prodigal son described in Luke 15:11-32, is waiting patiently for you to return to Him—and when you arrive at your heavenly home, He will be so excited to see you. God will announce a celebration of all celebrations, and you will be the object of His eternal joy.

A TENUOUS HOPE VERSUS
A CERTAIN TRUTH

RANDY ALCORN
Bestselling Author, *Heaven*

*The vague and tenuous hope that God is too kind to punish the ungodly
has become a deadly opiate for the consciences of millions. It hushes their
fears and allows them to practice all pleasant forms of iniquity while
death draws every day nearer and the command to repent goes unheeded.*
A. W. TOZER

In *The Knowledge of the Holy*, a book that profoundly impacted me
when I came to Christ as a teenager, Tozer speaks of the attributes
of God, including those we're tempted to minimize. Whether we
affirm the holiness and justice of God—and the doctrine of hell,
which is inseparable from them—may be the biggest test of
whether the Bible or our culture is our true authority.

Without hell, perpetrators of evil throughout the ages would
get away with every contemptible deed. But even if we acknowledge hell as a necessary punishment for evildoers, we rarely see
ourselves as deserving it. After all, *we* are not Hitler, Stalin or Mao.
(Are we?)

God responds, "There is no one righteous, not even one. . . .
All have turned away, they have together become worthless; there
is no one who does good, not even one" (Romans 3:10-12, *NIV*).

We consider ourselves good people.

We are dead wrong. To see the face of evil, we need only look in the mirror.

When most people speak of what a terrible notion hell is, they act as if it involves the suffering of innocent people. But nowhere does the Bible suggest that the innocent will spend even a moment in hell! Tozer wrote, "What comes into our minds when we think about God is the most important thing about us." Many modern Christians have reduced Him to a single-attribute God. Never mind that the angels in God's presence do not cry out, day and night, "Love, love, love," but "Holy, holy, holy is the LORD Almighty" (Isaiah 6:3, *NIV*).

By all means, we should rejoice in God's mercy and love. But we must also recognize that our Lord is relentlessly holy, righteous and just. "Your eyes are too pure to look on evil; you cannot tolerate wrong" (Habakkuk 1:13, *NIV*).

I have spoken at length with a few Christian writers who have reinvented the "good news." They see it not as an offer to be saved from everlasting punishment, but as an assurance that every person, regardless of whether they trust Christ in this life, will spend eternity in heaven. They rob the gospel of its stakes and urgency. They imagine they're paying God a compliment for being so tolerant, but it's not our job to airbrush Him or give Him a facelift.

Ironically, an exclusive emphasis on love strips God's love of its wonder. Without an understanding of the reality and consequences of sin, people aren't surprised by the idea that God loves them—why shouldn't He? But Scripture regards His love for us as remarkable, precisely because of our sin: "God demonstrates His own love toward us, in that while we were still sinners, Christ died for us" (Romans 5:8).

When John Newton wrote the hymn "Amazing Grace," he understood what made God's grace amazing—he was a hell-deserving "wretch." When we minimize our sinfulness, we minimize the power and wonder of God's grace. We undermine what God redeemed us for: "in order that in the coming ages he might show the incomparable riches of his grace, expressed in his kindness to us in Christ Jesus" (Ephesians 2:7, *NIV*).

What Tozer said 50 years ago could have been written last week:

A lot of people have talked about the goodness of God and then gotten sentimental about it and said, "God is too good to punish anybody," and so they have ruled out hell. But the man who has an adequate conception of God will not only believe in the love of God, but also in the holiness of God. . . . So let's not write dreamy poetry about the goodness of our heavenly Father who is love—"love is God and God is love and love is all in all and all is God and everything will be OK." That's the summation of a lot of teaching these days. But it's false teaching.[1]

Tozer saw clearly what we need to see. God has already composed his message—it's called the Bible. He doesn't need speechwriters, editors and PR people. He needs faithful messengers.

Though hell is dreadful, it is not evil. Hell is moral, because a good God must punish evil.

Some say, "Maybe hell exists, but surely it's not eternal."

Jesus said, "Then they will go away to eternal punishment, but the righteous to eternal life" (Matthew 25:46, *NIV*). Christ uses the same Greek word for "eternal" (*aionos*) to describe the duration of both heaven and hell.

The increasingly popular doctrine of annihilation merely confirms what most unbelievers already think—that their lives end at death, and therefore no judgment awaits them. We can certainly understand the appeal of such an expectation, but the fact is that Jesus spoke repeatedly of an eternal hell, describing unquenchable fires and the worm that never dies (see Mark 9:48).

In Luke 16:19-31, Jesus taught that an unbridgeable chasm separates hell from paradise. The wicked remain conscious, retain their memories, long for relief, cannot leave their torment, and are offered no hope. Our Savior couldn't have painted a bleaker picture.

Atheist Bertrand Russell wrote, "There is one very serious defect to my mind in Christ's moral character, and that is that He believed in hell. I do not myself feel that any person who is really profoundly humane can believe in everlasting punishment."[2]

Shall we trust Jesus or Bertrand Russell? For me, this is not a difficult choice.

If there isn't an eternal hell, or no one will end up there, Jesus made a huge mistake. If we cannot trust Jesus' teaching about hell, why should we trust anything else He said, including His offer of salvation?

We may pride ourselves in thinking we're too loving to believe in hell. But it's not loving to be silent when people are told the lie that they don't need to turn to Christ in this lifetime to be saved. Are we claiming to be more loving than Jesus, who with outrageous love bore the horrific penalty for our sin?

The Bible speaks of an eternal hell as something that should motivate unbelievers to turn to God, and believers to share the gospel with urgency.

By denying hell, we deny the extent of God's holiness. Worse yet, we deny the magnificence of God's grace. If the evils He died for aren't big enough to warrant eternal punishment, then perhaps the grace He showed us on the cross isn't big enough to warrant eternal praise.

The more we believe in *all* of God's attributes, including not only love and grace but also holiness and justice, the more hell will make sense to us.

Tozer wrote, "Death fixes the status of the man who loved his sins and he is sent to the place of the rejected where there is for him no further hope. That is hell, and it may be well we know so little about it. What we do know is sufficiently terrifying."[3]

If we are as loving as we claim, we'd better learn to speak Christ's truth in love—telling people that if they reject the best gift of a holy and gracious God, purchased with His own blood, what remains, in the end, will be nothing but hell.

Notes

1. A. W. Tozer and David E. Fessenden, *The Attributes of God, Volume 1: A Journey into the Father's Heart* (Camp Hill, PA: WingSpread, 2003), pp. 107-108.
2. Bertrand Russell, *Why I Am Not a Christian and Other Essays on Religion and Related Subjects*, edited by Paul Edwards (New York: Touchstone, 1967), p. 17.
3. A. W. Tozer, *God Tells the Man Who Cares* (Camp Hill, PA: WingSpread, 1992), p. 39.

28

THE PROBLEM WITH TRUTH

SUSAN PERLMAN
Founding Member and Associate Executive Director, Jews for Jesus

The truth resolves some difficulties and creates others.
A. W. TOZER

When people ask, "Why don't Jewish people believe in Jesus?" I'm tempted to give a host of historical and missiological facts to help them understand why my people are gospel-resistant. But usually people don't have that much time, and I find the short answer is all that most require: "For the same reason that most Gentiles don't believe in Him. It means telling God 'You're right and I'm wrong. I can't do anything to make myself right other than accept Your grace and forgiveness.'" And that's the truth.

In the Hebrew Scriptures, the word "truth" (*emet*) occurs 120 times. In most cases, it means support, stability or reliability. The New Testament usage (in Greek, *aletheia*) deals more with factuality and reality. When we study the Gospel of John, we find that truth is often not merely contrasted with falseness, but also presented as that which is complete (versus incomplete), definitive (versus provisional), and full (versus partial). These are not competing ideas of truth; they are like strands of a cord, and our understanding of truth is stronger when we take all these aspects into account. Just as truth is a multifaceted reality, the effects and consequences of truth are also multifaceted.

When Jesus pronounces, "I am the way, the truth, and the life" and follows it up with the statement, "No one comes to the Father except through Me" (John 14:6), He has resolved the primary difficulty of the human race: How do we come to the Father when our sin has separated us from Him? That is the issue at hand for people of every nation and background. We know this issue applies to all peoples, because Jesus spoke these words to Jewish people—heirs of the promises of God and partakers in the covenant. If anyone would be able to get around the "Jesus gate" to gain entrance to the Father, it would have been the very ones to whom Jesus was speaking when He said NO ONE comes to the Father but by Him.

We live in a time when many people are motivated by wishful thinking. We'd like to hope that there is enough truth in other religions that people can come to the Father by them. We want to believe that there is another way—or that somehow even though Jesus is the way, some have stumbled onto that way without ever knowing that it was Jesus or confessing Him as Savior.

There are some truths that are comfortable—like, "God loves you"—and other truths that are uncomfortable—like, "He expects you to go out and witness to your neighbors." Too often, our practice of religion has involved surrounding ourselves with comfortable truths and leaving the uncomfortable truths out on the periphery of our existence. But it sometimes takes those unpleasant truths to motivate us and energize us. The problem, when we draw comfortable truths all around us and push the uncomfortable truths far away, is that we immobilize ourselves beneath a pile of spiritual pillows. We become static because we're unchallenged, and we become still because we're not exercised.

So far as truth goes, the world lives by an illusion. That poses problems for us, because if we tell people that Jesus is who He claimed to be, those who don't receive Him will think of us as the antithesis of "pc"—narrow-minded, arrogant and, worst of all (as far as many are concerned), judgmental. As Tozer says, the assurance we have in Christ will be interpreted as bigotry. As those of us who routinely share the gospel know, we will also be scapegoated as the cause of conflict, and we will be utterly misunderstood . . . as Jesus was.

That is because the nature of truth is not to be comfortable but to be true—and while the truth sets us free, sometimes that very freedom obligates us to go where we'd rather not go and say what we'd rather not say. In fact, God has called us to wade through a world of rejection, just like He did, in order to find and to feed those who are genuinely hungry for truth.

I chose this particular quotation of Tozer's to write about because, to me, it has the feeling of an old Jewish proverb and conveys the tension that is found in so many of the great wisdom sayings. It shows me that as great and godly a man as Tozer was, he understood the nitty-gritty challenges we face. We can take heart in knowing, as he certainly did, that while the truth creates some problems for those of us who are committed to it, those problems are temporary, whereas the resolution it brings is eternal and glorious.

29

STRAIGHT RIVER

PAUL CLARK
Musician, Producer and Worship Leader

When people sugarcoat Christianity, arrange it all very nicely,
they have, in effect, taken away the Cross.
A. W. TOZER

Rudely awakened by a sudden drop in altitude, I instantly sought to combat my disorientation by merging the outside view with the inside mood of my fellow travelers.

"Everything is fine, just unexpected turbulence," the pilot proclaimed with the assurance of a Commander-in-Chief. Settling back in my seat, I returned my gaze to the agricultural tapestry blanketing the plains. Decades of vocational air travel had long since lessened my inclination to be a passionate observer of the ever-changing majestic topography beneath me. Suddenly, I now found myself scanning the squares and circles like a red-tailed hawk pursuing dinner.

Although the perimeters were congruent, my attention was drawn to the incongruent lines carved inside of each boundary. My songwriting skills were immediately summoned to scratch my visual itch . . .

I've never seen a straight river, flowing from the land or the sea; Up and down and all around, God's finger seems to carve them all with ease; so why do some people and some preachers on TV try to tell the world that God's so straight and neat?

I've never seen a square mountain, rising from the coast or the plains, Up and down and all around, God's finger never carves them all the same, why do some people and some preachers on TV try to tell the world that God's so straight and neat?

The sun in the sky every morning, it never looks the same from day to day, could this be a lesson, or a warning, the power of our God cannot be tamed? Beyond every star in creation, beyond every thought that one could dream, it takes a Divine imagination to build a plan for man to be redeemed, 'cause the star of His creation in that garden took a spill, so He sent His Son to die on Calvary's hill.

I've never seen a crooked sinner, that couldn't be forgiven from his shame; up and down and all around, God's finger carved my heart with Jesus' name; I'm a crooked sinner saved by grace and mercy, His Word has come, His truth has set me free . . . I've never seen a straight river.

I'll never be convicted for not being a forward-thinking disciple. In 1970, my "Hand to the Plow" calling was birthed in the basement of the Jesus Movement Hospital—where our electric guitars and drums provoked some church traditionalists to seek a way to "abort" me and a few other Contemporary Christian Music pioneers.

In the years since that time, as I've attempted to follow God's divine map in my own music ministry, I've had a birds-eye view of an increasing number of "hot house" worship farms. Consciously or obliviously, some of these corporate-run communities of faith pour enormous amounts of time and resources into manufacturing a larger-than-life hybrid gospel that grows in synthetic soil under thundering clouds of humidified fury that provide lightning, but no rain. It's delusional to think that copy-and-paste, "straight river" canal water, with sugar-sweetened Jesus bubbles, will transform the landscape of a dark and convoluted world the way a mighty rushing wind did in Jerusalem two millennia ago.

Perhaps equally alarming is the growing number of "believers" who resemble the children of Israel, wandering from barn to barn with their murmuring refrain: "What are we to drink?" (Exodus 15:24, *NIV*). Only a few days removed from witnessing Pharaoh's army drowned by the unlimited imagination of the living God, they became complaining nomads blind to the "I AM" GPS leading them to the pools of Marah. Until Moses' tree-casting obedience turned the bitter waters sweet, the Israelites failed to see that their sugarcoated, three-day sucker, filled with the truth-rotting decay of disobedience, was insufficient nutrition for traversing the Sinai Desert.

Unless we throw the testimony of Jesus' redemptive work on "the tree" into the selfish, bitter pools of our lives and the culture surrounding us, it's unlikely we will see any eternal fruit on the landscape anytime soon. Transformation is messy. As an encouragement, don't allow your "in-progress growth" to be stunted by fear or a sense of imperfection. The cross of Christ is more than sufficient to empower you to be His witness (see Acts 1:8).

We live in a world rapidly intent on modifying, and even eliminating, the cross of Christ. May you bypass the straight river and travel the winding, narrow road that offers endless opportunities for His grace to be proclaimed to all! "Even if our gospel is veiled, it is veiled to those who are perishing" (2 Corinthians 4:3).

30

AWARENESS OF
THE DIVINE

SCOTT SMITH
On-Air Host, K-LOVE Radio

What good is our busy religion if we've lost majesty, reverence,
worship—an awareness of the divine?
A. W. TOZER

This wisdom A. W. Tozer penned years ago is timeless and so applicable to what we face within the Church today. I think we sometimes forget that our faith is not designed to be like a trip to Target, where we get to pick and choose what we want to throw into our Christian shopping carts and leave what we don't want sitting on the shelves. We are making the Christian faith all about us, and not what God intended it to be: our lives given—surrendered—to Him and His plans. Psalm 148:13-14 says, "Let them praise the name of GOD—it's the only Name worth praising. His radiance exceeds anything in earth and sky; he's built a monument—his very own people!" (*THE MESSAGE*).

What I love most about A. W. Tozer's writing is its heart and authenticity. In a world that celebrates education and ever-growing knowledge, it is refreshing that a man with no more than an elementary education speaks with such wisdom—wisdom that could only be imparted by the Holy Spirit at work in his life. This is why Tozer's writings are so stirring to those who read them.

My first experience with Tozer was reading *The Pursuit of God*—a refreshing book that flies in the face of the society in which we live. Our culture is increasingly narcissistic—consumed with the "if it feels good, do it" mentality, which sadly has invaded our "pursuit of God." If you aren't careful, you can be tempted to treat your relationship with God like some sort of cheap consumerism, falling victim to the idea that God is here to make much of you, when in reality, you and I are created to make much of Him.

Don't get me wrong: I am not saying that trusting God doesn't come with its benefits. There are amazing promises that God bestows upon us, not the least of which is the promise of eternal life—fulfilled through God's gift of His only begotten Son, Jesus. Ephesians 1:3-6 says:

> How blessed is God! And what a blessing he is! He's the Father of our Master, Jesus Christ, and takes us to the high places of blessing in him. Long before he laid down earth's foundations, he had us in mind, had settled on us as the focus of his love, to be made whole and holy by his love. Long, long ago he decided to adopt us into his family through Jesus Christ. (What pleasure he took in planning this!) He wanted us to enter into the celebration of his lavish gift-giving by the hand of his beloved Son (*THE MESSAGE*).

Similarly, in 2 Corinthians 9:8-11 we read:

> God can pour on the blessings in astonishing ways so that you're ready for anything and everything, more than just ready to do what needs to be done. As one psalmist puts it, "He throws caution to the winds, giving to the needy in reckless abandon. His right-living, right-giving ways never run out, never wear out." This most generous God who gives seed to the farmer that becomes bread for your meals is more than extravagant with you. He gives you something you can then give away, which grows into full-formed lives, robust in God, wealthy in every way, so that

you can be generous in every way, producing with us great praise to God (*THE MESSAGE*).

My prayer is that the heart of Psalm 116 is something you hold on to with everything you have within you:

What can I give back to GOD for the blessings he's poured out on me? I'll lift high the cup of salvation—a toast to God! I'll pray in the name of GOD; I'll complete what I promised GOD I'd do, and I'll do it together with his people. When they arrive at the gates of death, GOD welcomes those who love him. Oh, GOD, here I am, your servant, your faithful servant: set me free for your service! (vv. 12-16, *THE MESSAGE*).

31

A CONTAGIOUS FIRE

ROBERT WHITT
Senior Pastor, Family Life Church, Elgin, Illinois

If worship bores you, you are not ready for heaven!
A. W. TOZER

In John 4:23-24, Jesus says, "But the hour is coming, and now is, when the true worshipers will worship the Father in spirit and truth; for the Father is seeking such to worship Him. God is Spirit, and those who worship Him must worship in spirit and truth" (John 4:23-24). There's an old saying: "You cannot kindle a fire in any other heart until it is burning within your own." Well, it's burning in mine.

How can anyone who has fallen in love with Jesus Christ and has a true relationship with Him be bored with worshiping the Father? "Let us come before him with thanksgiving [an act of giving thanks, an expression] and extol [to praise highly] him with music and song" (Psalm 95:2, *NIV*). "Serve the LORD with gladness; come before Him with joyful singing. Enter His gates with thanksgiving and His courts with praise" (Psalm 100:2,4, *NASB*).

People who love and have a true relationship with Jesus experience newfound freedom from sin, which gives them a fresh revelation of His truth that can't do anything but make them excited about worshiping Him!

When you have that type of experience, you become contagious—your enthusiasm infects everyone around you! It seems like the Church today is more concerned with wealth, health and happiness, as if comfort and luxury are the measuring stick for a successful life. Why is there such a lukewarm spirit when it comes to being enthusiastic about God? It seems like the announcement of a Super Bowl party after church service gets a more enthusiastic response than a pastor who has to pull teeth to get people to stand up and lift their hands before Jesus in praise.

In 1 Corinthians 14:40, the apostle Paul speaks about order in church meetings, saying, "Let all things be done decently and in order." Could the Church have misinterpreted what Paul was saying? The desire to keep things "decent and in order" has replaced the manifestation of life with a display of ceremony. As someone once said, "The only place in the community where everything is kept 'decent and in order' is the cemetery!"

The Church is not a place for the burial of the dead; it is a place for the living to celebrate Jesus Christ in freedom, which should generate spiritual enthusiasm!

As long as the Church (the Church being we who are believers in Jesus) feels like worship is a "duty," it will never inspire enthusiasm! However, when we become enthusiastic about Jesus Christ, worship will never be a mere duty. It will become a contagious expression that releases our emotions, blesses our God and affects those around us!

"Your kingdom come. Your will be done on earth as it is in heaven" (Matthew 6:10). In other words, if there is no boredom in worshiping God in heaven, then there shouldn't be any boredom in worshiping Him here on earth! If you think it's a little crazy on earth to worship God, wait until you get to heaven! It's really going to be off the charts! If you want that contagious spiritual effect—if you don't want to be bored in your worship—then get with a flock that rocks!

32

TO FIND GOD'S WILL, DO GOD'S WILL

GREGG MATTE
Senior Pastor, Houston's First Baptist Church

The man or woman who is wholly or joyously surrendered to Christ can't make a wrong choice—any choice will be the right one.
A. W. TOZER

We know where Moses was when God called to him. We know how old he was and what his past held. But maybe more important than any of these things is what Moses was doing when he encountered the burning bush: *nothing remarkable.* He was tending his father-in-law's flock, like he had done every day for half his life or more. Shepherding was his regular routine, and he was faithfully doing his job. Leading the flock to this area of the mountain was undoubtedly not a special occasion for Moses but something he did regularly, for shepherds often moved their flocks as the seasons changed and grazing conditions varied. He had almost certainly been on the backside of this mountain before.

Did you notice that Moses didn't even have his own sheep? They belonged to his father-in-law. Nothing remarkable there, for sure; he was on the backside of a mountain watching someone else's flock. But somehow he was ripe for God's choosing. The stage was being set. This was going to be a day of unexpected change. The hinge was about to swing on the "before" and "after" of Moses' life.

Today could be that same kind of day for you. God is not looking to elevate the already elevated. He is looking to tell a story—a story of the greatness of His plan, not a story about our skill. This week, a relational intersection could change the course of your life. A conversation on bended knee could be the tipping point of your prayer life. By the same token, an unexpected phone call could bring you to your knees in grief. Life isn't always easy, and its course can change in seconds, even as we try to plan out the years. What Jesus said in Matthew 6:34 is true: "Do not worry about tomorrow, for tomorrow will worry about itself. Each day has enough trouble of its own" (*NIV*).

Often we imagine that God's will is "out there" somewhere, 90 miles ahead of us and hidden like a needle in a haystack. But for Moses it was very close and not hidden at all. Each step tending his father-in-law's sheep in Nowheresville was a step closer to discovery. In fact, God helped him see it by calling attention to it, just in case he might have passed it by. He caused an ordinary bush to burn in an attention-getting way and appeared to Moses within the flame, calling him by name.

You might say, "I'd stop too if I saw a little self-starting bonfire like that, or if I heard God audibly speak my name." But would you, like Moses, be faithful in doing the thing that God has put before you to do when He calls?

The best way to *find* the will of God is to *do* the will of God. Let me offer an example to bring this home. How do you find God's will for career endeavors? First, you walk with integrity in all your dealings at work and you walk with a generous heart. You offer grace and understanding to your coworkers and colleagues, knowing that human beings make mistakes and that we're all in need of God's grace. When you walk out your faith each day at work in a godly fashion, you'll find that God will arrive before you do and show you the next step you're to take. Hard work and honesty are always in demand, regardless of the economy. Being the kind of employee that employers dream of puts usable material in the Lord's hands. He is the best agent a faithful job hunter can hope for.

How do you find someone to marry or improve your existing marriage? You walk with purity, as the Bible teaches. You become the kind of person you want to be married to. Are you looking for someone kind? Then grow in kindness. Are you looking for someone responsible? Then pay your bills on time. Are you looking for your spouse to be a person of prayer? Then hit your knees. Become the person to whom you want to be married. Godliness is not a luxury or a bonus in a dating relationship or marriage (see 2 Corinthians 6:14); it's a requirement. If you are a Christian and intend to obey God and marry a Christian, then you need to be dating a Christ-follower. If you are married and desire greater godliness in your spouse, step it up yourself. By doing God's will, you take a step further in finding His will. A German proverb sums it up: "Begin to weave, and God will give you the thread."

Too many times we stand dead still at a fork in the road, refusing to move and pleading for God to show us the way. But He is saying, "If you will just walk with Me, I will show you." The best way to *find* the will of God is to *do* the will of God. Mark Twain is alleged to have once said, "It ain't those parts of the Bible that I can't understand that bother me; it is the parts that I do understand." We already know much in our core about what is right and what is wrong. By living what we know, God is preparing us to live what we don't yet know. We can't do multiplication until we learn addition.

We prepare for the future by doing the next right thing. As Tommy Nelson says, "God hits moving targets." Doing God's will leads to discovering God's will. Each step on the mountainside of faith is a step closer to your burning bush. Even if you have someone else's sheep in tow on the far side of town, God may have a life-changing intersection for you just around the next bend.

33

FROM MOURNING TO DANCING

KIRSTEN HAGLUND

Miss America 2008 and Member of Sean Hannity's
Great American Panel

*The Bible was written in tears,
and to tears it yields its best treasures.*
A. W. TOZER

In Las Vegas, Nevada, in January 2008, I received the title and job of "Miss America." For the next year, I would travel around the country (logging as many as 20,000 miles a month), receive beautiful gowns from the best designers, speak to lawmakers on Capitol Hill, sign countless autographs and make daily television appearances. This would have been a dream come true for many young women.

However, at 19 years old, I had spent the past year in college and had simply entered a local pageant to earn scholarship money for school. I had also very recently managed to recover physically from a battle with anorexia nervosa, with which I had begun struggling at the age of 12. At the time that I won Miss America, I felt nervous, but ready—unsure, but full of faith and optimism. I felt confident that I was strong enough to make it through the year, and I would do the best job that I could.

I was in no way prepared for the spiritual battle that would follow during that year of "service." I soon realized that while I had broken many of the behaviors of my eating disorder, the roots of the illness remained. The fact was that I had a much deeper disorder—a worship disorder. During my year as Miss America, I was highly scrutinized and held to an unachievable high standard of beauty, intelligence, style, weight and personality. Everyone I encountered had an idea of what Miss America should be—and many had the courage and pluck to tell me I wasn't it.

A desire to serve and glorify the Lord every day was replaced by a desire to please man. Approval of the "job" I was doing and my appearance again became equated with self-worth. Isolation from family, friends and my church community didn't help. I thought I was striving for perfection in order to please and worship God—when really I was worshiping and seeking the approval of the world.

What an astonishing and crushing realization! By November 2008, I was exhausted. I was broken, lost and desperate for God's Word. I longed for something real—for some truth. In a world filled with glossy images, political correctness and the "American Ideal," I thirsted for something more; I desperately wanted someone to crawl into the pit of despair in which I found myself and rescue me.

I remember lying facedown on the floor in a hotel room in San Diego, crying out to the Lord for wisdom. I arose and opened my Bible to Jeremiah 31:3-4—the pages fell open naturally to a verse I'd often read, but this time, as I read it through my tears, the Holy Spirit moved: "I have loved you with an everlasting love; therefore I have continued my faithfulness to you. Again I will build you, and you shall be built, O virgin Israel! Again you shall adorn yourself with tambourines and shall go forth in the dance of the merrymakers" (*ESV*). The promise of these words, written by the "weeping prophet," touched my heart, and I was reminded of the goodness of Christ.

I flipped to the Psalms and vowed to read every morning one of those songs of David, written in tears. Slowly, through His Word, Christ pulled me out of the pit of depression and despair.

Through the Holy Spirit, the Scriptures that had been penned by tearful men convicted a sinner of her selfishness and pride. But for this daughter of Christ, His Scripture also caused me to dance for joy at the freedom that comes through repentance and grace. Let us cling like small children to the hope that is found in His Word, which alone restores the broken, renews our hearts, and helps us to rejoice in our Maker.

34

GRATITUDE IS MORE THAN A FEELING

TED TRAVIS
Associate Pastor, Lawndale Community Church, Chicago, Illinois

Gratitude is an offering precious in the sight of God,
and it is one that the poorest of us can make and be
not poorer but richer for having made it.
A. W. TOZER

Have you ever been profoundly grateful? I mean deeply, astonishingly, awe-inspiringly grateful? I thank God for all His many blessings. But—perhaps because I have some years under my belt—I can highlight a few that stir within me an especially deep and profound gratitude.

Salvation is a biggie. It was 37 years ago that I sat down with Bud after church and prayed to receive Christ. I now look back with joy on the inner transformations God has wrought in my life since that moment: the capacity to love, appreciate and serve others. I lean daily on God's mercy, His constant forgiveness and cleansing from sin. Inspired indeed are the lyrics from "My Tribute" by Andrae Crouch:

> The voices of a million angels could not express
>   my gratitude.

All that I am and ever hope to be, I owe it all to Thee.
To God be the glory.

Another is my wife, Shelly. There are moments when I just stop
and gaze at her; I can still see the beautiful young girl I married 30
years ago. Entrusting herself to a man for life, even with God's
help, is an amazing act of trust and vulnerability for any woman.
To this day, I remain in awe that she gave herself to me. I am profoundly grateful.

Such gratitude can be striking in its expression. I have been
part of the Christian Community Development Association since
it began in 1989. Over the years, this organization has birthed rich
ministry partnerships and life-long friendships, not the least of
which is a special friendship with its founder, John Perkins. John
is a man characterized by profound gratitude; you cannot listen
to him without being arrested by his sincere thankfulness for
friends, family and salvation. It consumes him; he seems forever
amazed by the greatness of God's love.

As John and others would attest, real gratitude goes beyond
feeling. "Sacrifice thank offerings to God, fulfill your vows to the
Most High, and call upon me in the day of trouble; I will deliver
you, and you will honor me" (Psalm 50:14-15, NIV). The psalmist
is saying that religious posturing is meaningless; what counts to
God is genuine, heart-felt gratitude. But then, in the same breath,
the psalmist speaks of vows, or promises. There is a connection
between thankfulness and service. Genuine gratitude, it seems,
evokes a corresponding response.

John Perkins often says, "God loves me, and now I spend my
life loving God back." My gratitude for the gift of Shelly also
evoked such a response. I have intentionally sought over the years
to be there for her, to love her with God's love, to nurture that marvelous fun-loving spirit, and to preserve through faithful encouragement her unique zest for life.

Years ago, a young man immersed in gang life responded to
the grace of God. He broke free from the culture of the streets with
a desire to help youth still trapped within that culture discover

new life in Christ. He fulfilled that desire under my tutelage on staff with our ministry. One day I gave him a charge—a challenge from one redeemed inner-city Christian leader to another:

> Jimmy, the kids in this neighborhood know you. They know your family and they know your past. Many are immersed in the lifestyle you once had. They're asking a simple question: *What can God do with the likes of someone like me?* They're asking, all the while looking at you. The answer they receive will be influenced in no small measure by what they see God doing in your life.

Gratitude goes beyond feeling. My challenge to Jimmy—and this is the same thing I often ask of myself—was this: "How will you respond to the grace of God? When kids look at you, what will they see? *Just how grateful are you?*"

There are things for which I am profoundly grateful: deeply, astonishingly, awe-inspiringly grateful. Gratitude enriches the one who experiences it, but apparently it doesn't end there. God has a way of getting great mileage out of it—and that can bless even the poorest among us.

To God be the glory!

35

The Importance of Getting a Good Start

JENN GOTZON
Award-winning Actress, *Frost/Nixon, Doonby, God's Country* and *I Am . . . Gabriel*

Sometimes when we get overwhelmed we forget how big God is.
A. W. TOZER

It's amazing how easy it is to sprint out of bed when the alarm goes off, brush your teeth, do the shower-and-get-ready thing, rush out the door, hit traffic and plead, "God, please help me get there in time," arrive in the nick of time and begin another series of events—and then come home exhausted and stressed. Only if we pause to reflect do we realize that we went through the entire day in our *own* strength and *own* power, even though we have a heavenly Father who yearns to walk with us daily. Our God is eager to give us an endless provision of guidance and *His* supernatural strength and power—which consistently provides a peace that surpasses understanding and a more efficient direction for each day . . . if we quiet ourselves, talk to God and listen.

When I start each morning reading the Bible and spending time in prayer, I experience God intimately in my soul throughout the day. When I don't, I feel overwhelmed by the day's struggles. Here's a snapshot of my daily routine of spending time with

God—embracing how big He truly is—which I share only to help those who may not know how to pray:

1. I pray for God to open my heart so I may hear His voice. In the movie *I Am . . . Gabriel*, the characters kneel on a prayer mat, which reminds them that God wants them to talk to Him, and that He hears and answers their prayers.

2. I read the day's devotion in the book *Jesus Calling* by Sarah Young. My mother-in-law gave me this devotional while I was filming *Doonby*. This has been a beautiful blessing to my mom and me in helping us experience God during our morning devotions.

3. I spend time reading the Bible. I like to read the entire chapter that corresponds with the Scripture verses for that day in *Jesus Calling*.

4. In my journal, I write out praises to God for His goodness, grace and *His* magnificent creation. I seek forgiveness and ask for guidance for any areas of struggle, pray for family and friends' needs, and then continue writing—listening to hear God's voice and guidance. When I was going to school for acting in New York City, my friend Laura and her mom taught me how to hear God. Having a conversation requires us not only to talk to God but also to be still and listen. Just like how we build a relationship with a friend by talking and listening.

5. I finish my prayer time by asking God for *His* strength, guidance, peace, protection, wisdom and joy for the day. One time when I was serving as a greeter for a big industry event at the church I was attending, I was really tired and depressed. I asked God to fill me with

joy and strength, and by the end of the evening, I couldn't believe the supernatural power with which the Lord's spirit filled me. It reminded me how big God truly is!

It's a fascinating paradigm shift of supernatural perspective when we begin to understand how much God loves us and how much He wants to be intimately with us throughout the day. When we spend time talking with Him on our knees, face down on a prayer mat, cozied up with our Bible or driving down the road in prayer—any which way—God will continue to reveal how big He truly is when we draw near to Him.

36

THE SPEAKING WORD

BODIE AND
BROCK THOENE

Authors of the *A.D. Chronicles* and the *Zion Covenant*

Until the Bible begins to talk to us, we really have not been reading it.
A. W. TOZER

Those of us who believe the Bible is the Holy Spirit-inspired, infallible Word of God often pat ourselves on the back for our wisdom in holding that position.

We congratulate ourselves for knowing that the Bible is more than myth or legend or philosophy or moral platitudes.

Yet we still manage to miss the bigger picture.

Many of us who love Scripture are so eager to capture "Bible knowledge" that we learn to outline and subdivide it into recognizable categories: law, history, poetry and prophecy. We can locate the Sermon on the Mount, we know where Paul teaches on love, and we are able to quote John 3:16.

Still, we fail to understand that the Bible is a love letter, written by the Creator of the universe and addressed to us personally. We don't recognize all the levels on which God's Word speaks. We neglect to re-explore what we believe is familiar material, not realizing that if we did, we would find new and exciting insights hidden there.

We have learned to quote, "For the word of God is living and active, sharper than any two-edged sword, piercing to the division of soul and of spirit, of joints and of marrow, and discerning the thoughts and intentions of the heart" (Hebrews 4:12, *ESV*), and on one level, we believe it.

But here's what too many of us fail to see: The Bible was written to real people—living human beings who were breathing, striving, failing, struggling, and experiencing joys and sorrows—just as we do today.

Nothing is included in Holy Scripture based on the flip of a scribe's coin. No Gospel author scratched his head and said, "I think I'll record this story about Jesus because it's as good as another I could choose."

No! Every word is selected with the same divine precision that orders the stars and the tides.

When Saint Luke uses the word "manger" over and over again in just 10 verses of chapter 2 of his Gospel, it isn't because he thinks his readers have short memories or attention spans. It's because the Spirit prompted him to instruct us: "Listen! Pay attention! This is important!"

Here's just part of that deeper picture. We read in the prophecy of Isaiah: "The ox knows its owner, and the donkey its master's crib" (Isaiah 1:3, *ESV*). This use of "crib" is synonymous with "manger." Have you ever wondered why nativity scenes always picture an ox and a donkey standing beside the manger? In a direct reference to Isaiah, the New Testament scene shows how mute animals recognize their Creator and Lord within the child in the manger—but that realization is not shared by the wider world of humans apart from the Holy Family, the magi, and the Temple shepherds.[1]

Once you begin to study every passage of Scripture with Tozer's attitude in the front of your thoughts, you will never read the Bible in the same way again. Once you begin to examine God's Word through the lens of asking yourself: "Why did the writer choose that particular phrase? Why did he select that story to tell? Why does he emphasize that single word over and over?" you will begin to peel back the centuries-old layers of cultural and historical overlay and come to see the Bible as alive and speaking personally to you today . . . and every day.

Note

1. For more on this imagery, see our Little Book of Why: *Why a Manger?*

37

DOING GREAT
THINGS FOR GOD

CECIL MURPHEY
Bestselling Author; Co-Author, *90 Minutes in Heaven*

We can be in our day what the heroes of faith were in their day—
but remember at the time they didn't know they were heroes.

A. W. TOZER

I once asked members of a Sunday School class, "How many of
you would like to do great things for God?"

All 21 students quickly and enthusiastically raised their
hands. I smiled and asked my next question: "How many of you
are willing to clean the floors here at church?"

They seemed puzzled by the question, but they raised their
hands again—much more slowly the second time.

A few years ago I taught homiletics at a Bible college. I asked
the first question this way: "How many of you would willingly
become the pastor of a 5,000-member congregation?" Every
hand went up.

"How many of you would choose to go to a church of 10
members?"

Not a hand went up; instead they asked questions, such as:
"Would there be growth potential?" and "Is it a new-church
development?"

I wanted to make the point that most of us would willingly become outstanding leaders for God. Not many would volunteer for the humble, unnoticed tasks.

Jesus stressed the negative side of that reality. Several times we read in the Gospels that the disciples argued among themselves over who would be greatest in the Kingdom. James and John put their mother up to asking Jesus to give her sons first place.

John 13:1-20 tells us that when the disciples met in an upper room, no one took on the lowly task of washing the others' feet. Jesus didn't rebuke or correct them. Instead, He got up and, with a basin of water and a towel, knelt in front of each disciple and washed the man's feet.

It's a rather astonishing story all around, but to me, the most amazing fact is that only Peter objected. Didn't it bother the rest that their leader became their servant?

Although we are familiar with this powerful object lesson, we in the Church still don't grasp the message. It's easy to ignore the greeter at the church door, the person who makes coffee, or the usher who is at church every Sunday. Those things need doing, but they still seem insignificant to us.

Yet as I read about the great heroes of the faith, they seemed to serve faithfully without any expectation of rewards of praise or being called heroes. In Acts 6, Peter asks the primitive Church to select seven men to serve food at the tables because the Greek-speaking Christians felt discriminated against.

We know what happened to two of those table servers. First, they faithfully served food, because that was their task. Not long afterward, one of them—a man named Stephen—testified boldly about Jesus. The leading Jews turned on him. Through the centuries, Christians have admired Stephen as the first martyr of the Christian faith. That puts him on the A-list, doesn't it?

Philip didn't do too badly, either. He evangelized the city of Samaria (see Acts 8) and later brought the message of salvation to a man from Ethiopia. We also read that his four daughters prophesied, so he must have taught them well. But he started out as a "lowly" waiter.

I doubt that Philip or Stephen ever thought of greatness or of ranking along with the apostles. They focused on doing what God called them to do at that stage of their lives.

Like them, we should have as our goal being faithful to the job; rewards and fame are God's choice.

38

WHAT LEADS TO LIFE

VINCE AND
MARYANN BARLOW
Musicians, Managers and Parents of the Barlow Girls

I pray that I will be willing to let my Christian experience and standards
cost me something right down to my last gasp.
A. W. TOZER

God has given us some impossible challenges in His Word. Consider, for example, the expectation for marriage: "They shall become one flesh" (Genesis 2:24). Ask anyone who has tried that just how easy that is. How about "Love your enemies . . . [and] do good to those who hate you" (Matthew 5:44)? Sounds nice on paper, but when I am challenged to do it in real life, I often fail or run away. But the hardest challenge God has ever given is to lay down our lives and die to our own desires (see Matthew 16:24; 1 John 3:16). We should not be surprised by this challenge. Anything of value that God calls us to involves death. It is just His way.

I have had a great teacher in my life, instructing me about love and sacrifice. My wife, MaryAnn, has taught me so much about love and the high cost of showing people they are loved. Our society is a very independent environment, encouraging us to adopt a "fend for yourself" way of life. MaryAnn has taught me that the only way we have value on the inside is if someone gives it to us by an act of sacrifice. True value only comes as a gift from someone who has paid a price for it.

My wife would lay down her life and go to the nth degree to love our children, and I would often say, "Why are you doing so much?" She would always reply, "The only way the children will never forget they are loved is if someone is willing to die to his or her own desires to meet their needs." When our children were babies and waking up in the middle of the night, I would say, "Let them cry if they're fed and dry." But MaryAnn would go and hold them to show them that their comfort was worth her sacrifice. She knew something far greater than I knew: that love only comes through someone dying—and that if she would die for her children, someday they would die for others. The fruit she desired in her children was that they would be people willing to lay down their lives for others. The price of that was her own "death."

When my wife and I were first married, we wanted to live lives that honored God and raise a family that would impact the world. Sounds heroic! Actually, all heroes have to risk their lives to become truly heroic. We prayed the prayer: *God, use our family to build Your Kingdom.* We figured He would be so happy about such a noble prayer that He would roll out the red carpet for us. Not quite! Instead, conviction started to come, and I wasn't happy. God called us to do one thing after another that we didn't want to do—things that were outside of our comfort zone.

From home birth to home school, to not replacing our TV antenna when it blew off the roof, to no R-rated movies and no teen magazines. Yes, my wife would take away any teen magazines she found our children reading and place Foxe's *Book of Martyrs* in their hands instead. "Read this," she would say. "You will become like the people you focus on." Bit by bit, God made it clear to us that if we wanted to raise children of His Kingdom—children who would change the world—then they could not look, think or act like the world. Needless to say, our flesh wasn't very happy with many of God's leadings. I was going to say God's "suggestions"— but God doesn't make suggestions. He leads, and we must choose whether to follow and move forward or not follow and just stay in the same place.

God also called us to die by having us lay down our pride and confess some of our past sins to our children—for instance, things we did before we were married. God didn't care that those things happened before we were Christians; He told us how powerful it would be if we confessed our sins and asked our children for forgiveness. We watched as our truth-telling broke the power of generational sin patterns and kept our children from walking in the same way. Though it was hard at first for us to burst the bubble of our parental image, the very things we have shared with our children have helped create places of strength in them that they would say are their greatest moral strengths. Through our being honest about how we had failed, they became very aware of the power of temptation and learned how to be strong and avoid the same sins.

As we get older, I have many regrets, most of them around seeing the imbalance between the abiding fruit that true acts of love brought about and the lack of fruit from many things I did in years of ministry for which I didn't have to die. There are people I "led to Christ" with a cheap faith method whose lives were never transformed by the power of the gospel. All the promises of the "good life" Jesus would bring to them never panned out. I gave them empty promises of a free gift with no strings attached, and most of them have discarded their faith. Where is the fruit? Fruit only grows in a field where someone was willing to pay a sacrificial price to cultivate and till and keep the garden. I love planting my garden in the spring. I don't like weeding my garden in the summer, but I have learned that when I do, I have an abundant harvest—and when I don't, I have a mess.

There is no way to show people that they are valuable unless you are willing to die for them.

39

CONTAGIOUS CHRISTIANS

BEN KASICA
Lead Guitarist, Skillet

There are rare Christians whose very presence incites others to be better Christians. I want to be that rare Christian.

A. W. TOZER

Many times in my life, another believer has entered a room I was in, and I could sense the presence of God on them—something about them was different. I instantly felt encouraged in my spirit. I believe, very simply, that those Christians are full of the Holy Spirit, living life in the Spirit as God intended.

When we live by the Spirit, we become a conduit of the grace of God to others. We operate with "charisma," which is the Latin translation of the Greek word *kharisma* or *kharis* (favor, grace), and the root of today's *Charismatic* (grace gift). When the Church operates in these "grace gifts," the effect is as Paul said: "Whenever you come together, each of you has a psalm, has a teaching, has a tongue, has a revelation, has an interpretation. Let all things be done for edification" (1 Corinthians 14:26). We are meant to encourage each other daily in the Spirit, whether by bringing a word of encouragement, a song, a prayer or prophecy. When we carry the anointing and grace of God in our lives, it is contagious. The benefits of His grace are not just meant for us; that grace is meant to flow out of us as a gift to others, bringing comfort, encouragement and, most importantly, revelation—all for God's glory.

So how does one become that type of Christian? God made it easy: simply be with Him. Seek Him. Fall in love with Him. You will be changed and become that contagious Christian who inspires others. When Moses went up on the mountain to meet with God, he was changed. He came back down with a new anointing, and even his outward appearance had noticeably changed (see Exodus 34:28-30). When we seek the Lord, He is faithful to change us, because God *is* love—and He loves us too much not to mold us and build us for His purposes. When we encounter God, we begin to take on His attributes—we become like Him.

Ever since I was young, my father has told me, "You shouldn't leave the house in the morning until you have had an encounter with God and are filled with the Holy Spirit. If you leave and are full of yourself, you're bringing yourself to others and not the Holy Spirit. You're ripping them off from what God wants to bring to them through you." It's radical, I know, but I've always been challenged by my father's exhortation in my daily life.

The sad truth is that many Christians don't access what's available to them through the Holy Spirit. For some, it's because they neglect time with God, while for others, it's a lack of revelation of what it means to be "full of the Holy Spirit." I know that I sometimes neglect that time with God because—well, for many reasons. I'm busy, this or that came up, I'm too tired, I'm too . . . you fill in the blank. Did you encounter God today? If not, why not? It is rare, as Tozer suggests, to come across those contagious Christians, but it shouldn't be. It should be normal.

God didn't send His Holy Spirit for a select few Christians to have that effect on others. He sent Him for all believers. He sent Him with limitless reserve, beckoning us to know Him in fullness—to encounter Him every day. We should not wait to enjoy mountaintop experiences from time to time; we should be living with and encountering God daily. We were created for this very thing—intimate fellowship with God. We lost this vital relationship in the fall, and we gained it back in the death and resurrection of Jesus. Knowing and worshiping God, walking with Him, being intimate with Him—our hungry hearts long for these things. When we live in the fullness of communion with God through the Holy Spirit, we become those "rare Christians whose very presence incites others to be better Christians"—not because we are trying to be that way, but because we are full of the Spirit and allow Him to work in our lives. It's effortless, yet powerful.

40

THE LAP OF
A FATHER

ABBIE SMITH
Author, *Can You Keep Your Faith in College?* and *The Slow Fade*

When I understand that everything happening to me is to make me more
Christlike, it solves a great deal of anxiety.
A. W. TOZER

Anxiety is all around us, and it affects every one of us. In subtle and serious ways, it intrudes on relationships and robs us of joy. It gnaws at our security and kneads away our peace. It collapses freedom and convinces us we are trapped in an unforgiven existence.

As Christians, though, we've been offered another way. God stepped out of heaven to expose a life simultaneously lived on earth and lived for the life beyond—and He invited us to follow. Everything that happens, then, in the life of the regenerate heart, holds an invitation. Everything that happens presents an opportunity for us to become more Christlike. Meaning, the silence, the miscarriage, the mistake, the divorce, the singleness, the car wreck, the cancer, the weight, the bill, the heartbreak, the death, the abuse, the traffic, the neighbor, the war, the job, the neglect, the dream, the fear, the exam, the president, the decision . . . not one of these happens without unthinkable empathy from Jesus Himself. And not one of these happens without redemptive invitation to further shape our views of self and God, whose infinite perspective and vision breaks through brokenness and restores ashes to beauty. When we realize that our days are aggressively shaped by our Savior, we understand that we're allowed to rest—to nestle deeply into the lap of a Father—a Father who cares for us, knows His plan for us, and leads our days accordingly. We realize that life is not a bunch of loose ends we must tie, or problems we must solve, but it's a profound, eternal tapestry that we are called to be *part of.*

If we are to call Scripture and Tozer's words *true* today, our question seems to boil down to one of kingdoms. Are we moving toward the arbitrary and chaotic kingdom in our midst, scrounging to alleviate its morbid end in death? Or are we moving toward the kingdom of God, sculpted for everlasting life?

To be Christlike is to become sanctified. To become sanctified is to believe that life is led by the Godhead, three-in-one, and that I've been invited to be *like Him.* To become sanctified is to loosen my grip on things formerly held firm, laying down control as the captain of my ship and master of my soul. To be Christlike, and thus to become sanctified, is to discover my humanity and the divinity of the One who dwells within.

For those of us who are followers of Jesus, the most fundamental part of our identity is not "anxiety." Rather, we are *chosen children of God, beloved* and *sought-after.* Therefore, we can have hope. Not only has God forgiven us and set us free, but He also delights in us, and in who we are becoming—as those who are like Him.

Thy Kingdom come, Thy will be done, on earth as it is in heaven.

41

FOOLISH THINGS

TORRY MARTIN

Actor, Comedian and Author

*Do not allow the enemy of your soul to rob you of that
unique quality God has breathed into you.*
A. W. TOZER

I was the kid who never fit in—literally. Desk chairs, cafeteria tables, bus seats—I viewed them all as medieval torture for rotund
teens. It wasn't just my weight, however, that kept me from "fitting
in." I was also non-athletic, socially awkward and a horrible student. But mostly I was invisible—or at least I felt that way.

My journal was my trusted confidant and best friend. I wrote
about being torn between wanting to be seen for myself and wanting to be anyone *but* myself. I enjoyed making comical observations about my peers and writing witty one-liners that I imagined
zinging my tormentors with. I would have put these remarks to
use if I hadn't been so afraid of getting stuffed into a locker. Or—
okay, let's be honest—*two* lockers.

I discovered acting in high school and found great consola-
tion in playing other characters. So after graduating, I moved to
California to pursue an acting career. My insecurities, however, led
me into activities I would later regret. I have termed that 10-year

period my "Decade of Sinning Dangerously." Eventually, disillusioned by my failures and tired of feeling foolish, I gave up on my dreams and moved back to Washington and the safety of my parents' house. The devil was robbing me, and I was allowing it. I eventually moved, of all places, to Alaska, taking up residence in a remote cabin amid 80 acres of protected wetlands. It was there that I asked Jesus to forgive me of my sins and become Lord of my life. I was happier than I'd ever been. I became part of a church family that I loved and that loved me back. The groundwork was laid: I was about to figure out that God actually had specifically laid plans for my life.

I began acting again, participating in several church productions, and I heard about a national talent competition called "Christian Artists' Seminar in the Rockies." My church took up a collection for me to go and compete—and before I knew it, I was in Colorado, accepting the grand prize for my performance.

I enjoyed winning the prize, but I felt like an imposter. I had a preconceived idea of what a Christian should be, and I didn't fit the mold. I knew I was forgiven for my past and that God loved me, but the enemy of my soul would often whisper to me that I was the dirtiest of sinners and, besides that, an awkward loser. So I simply accepted the award and returned quietly to my life as a hermit.

One day, while sitting in my little cabin watching TV, I heard something that changed my life. The words of the televangelist were simple but profound: "Exercising our gifts is a matter of obedience." The evangelist then quoted Romans 12:6: "Since we have gifts that differ according to the grace given to us, each of us is to exercise them accordingly" (*NASB*). He said that failure to exercise our gifts can adversely affect the Body of Christ—and the very glory of God.

That woke me from my spiritual stupor. Adversely affecting God's glory seemed like pretty serious business! I started an in-depth Bible study to find out all I could about spiritual gifts.

I discovered several things: First, spiritual gifts are gifts of God's grace (see Ephesians 3:7-8), even for those who feel like "the least of all God's people" (*NIV*)—as I did. God's *saving* grace assigns us places of *service* in His Kingdom. That was a real eye-opener. Next I learned that God gives us different personalities, temperaments and gifts (see Ephesians 4:11), and He uses them all to His glory. Surrender is the key! Then I found that our gifts are to be used in community (see Ephesians 4:12-13). They are for building up and unifying the Body. Using our gifts actually allows the Body of Christ to function properly (see Ephesians 4:16).

Suddenly I realized that it was completely unacceptable for me to live like a hermit, cut off from people. The entire Body of Christ depended on me to fulfill God's purpose for me! It was time for me to tell the devil to shut up, to embrace who God made me to be, and to get to work.

I went on to read a book that helped me deal with what the devil had stolen from me during my decade of sinning dangerously. That book was Tozer's *I Talk Back to the Devil*, and it was brilliant and life changing.

As if that wasn't enough, my pastor challenged me further. I often told funny stories around his table in Alaska, and Pastor Aiken encouraged me to add spiritual applications to the stories and tell them from the stage as myself, not as a character. "Pastor," I told him, "I'm more comfortable playing someone else. I don't think God can use me as a speaker because . . . I'm stupid."

Pastor Aiken paused for a moment and looked me in the eye. "Yes, you are." He very seriously completed his thought. "But you are *very* unique in your 'stupidity,' and God wants to use that."

Ha! Is that not the craziest thing ever? But it was a beautiful insult, and it greatly comforted me. For the first time, I saw that my awkwardness doesn't make me a loser—in fact, it's part of my gifting! It perfectly equips me to be sensitive to others and to make them laugh. I am "uniquely stupid"—and that, my friends, makes me a star!

I competed in the artists' seminar again the next year, and this time I tried my hand at writing sketches. I didn't know the difference between an adverb and a fraction, but somehow God allowed this kid who'd had a *D* average in high school to win a grand prize.

Then my first book of comedy sketches was published with Lillenas Drama. People started telling me I had "an ear for writing believable dialogue" and "a knack for creating characters." That's when I had a personal epiphany: All those seemingly wasted years I spent as a shy, socially awkward kid who kept a journal had been my training ground as a writer. God is good!

Paul McCusker, the producer of *Adventures in Odyssey*, noticed my work. He approached me about creating a character based on my "persona" (I didn't even know what a persona was!), and told me that the character would be "bumbling, bizarre, gullible and naïve." I was amazed. All through school I had hardly gotten one compliment, but now the Peabody Award-winning writer Paul McCusker had just given me four! It was exhilarating!

The devil had been wrong. "God has chosen the foolish things of the world to put to shame the wise" (1 Corinthians 1:27).

Don't let the devil lie to you. Don't let your insecurities or your past stop you. God needs your gifts, and if you withhold them, it affects His glory. Find your work of service. Follow your passion. Accept the gift of God. You'll never know what you're missing if you don't take a chance. All you have to do is say yes!

42

STRANGELY NORMAL

WES AND DAVID BEAVIS
Motivational Speaker (and Son)

Go to church once a week and nobody pays attention. Worship God seven days a week and you become strange!
A. W. TOZER

Halfway through the spring semester of my (David's) junior year of high school, a new student transferred to the school. On his first day, the vice principal was showing him around and brought him over to meet my friends and me. We took turns introducing ourselves to the new student. After I introduced myself, one of the guys in the group asked the new student if he was religious.

"Uh, no, not really. I mean, I am a little. Like my family and I go to church on Sunday sometimes, but other than that, nothing crazy."

"All right, that's cool. I was just asking 'cause David over here is kind of religious."

Well, that was me in high school. I was known as the "religious guy." I did not understand why. Most of my friends believed in God and identified themselves as Christians, but still, I was the "religious" one out of the group. (For the record, I do not like the term "religious"—but we'll get to that a little later.)

To be honest, I did not really have an interest in living my whole life for God up until my junior year of high school. Spending Sunday with Him seemed like enough for one week. However, by the grace of God, He started working within me and gave me the desire to live a life pleasing to Him—on more days than just Sunday. Because of this, my friends thought I was a little different—or, better yet, strange.

Herein lies the danger of Christianity being boxed into the term "religion." Jesus becomes simply a doctrine that one admires only on Sundays. At least, that is what I have often observed. But the beauty of the gospel is that we are not called into religion. We are called into relationship! Think about your best friend. Are you content with talking to that person only once a week for an hour and a half? If you said yes, then I would question whether that is an authentic relationship.

In Colossians 3:17, Paul writes: "And whatever you do, whether in word or deed, do it all in the name of the Lord Jesus, giving thanks to God the Father through him" (*NIV*). This verse does not designate a time, such as Sunday morning at 11 A.M., for doing everything "in the name of the Lord Jesus." How awesome is it that a relationship with the God of the Universe does not end after the dismissal of a church service?

So why does our society view worshiping God every day of the week as so abnormal? Maybe because we have obtained over the years a misunderstanding of what normal is. I (Wes) would go so far as to say that we have allowed the world to define what is "normal." The world has worked overtime to remove all elements of Christ from society. The remaining culture—stripped of Christian teaching and traditions—is proudly heralded as tolerant, diverse and "normal."

The reality is that the world has done a woeful job of creating "normal." Homicides, suicides, abortions, and children being subjected to unspeakable violence, abuse and neglect—sad to say— have become commonplace in our world today; these things have become normal. Meanwhile, being dedicated to the cause of Christ—seven days a week—is deemed by the world to be strange.

Who is calling whom crazy?! Let no Christian be intimidated by the world's definitions any longer. The world has hijacked normal and driven it into a ditch. The world's normal is not nicer, kinder or more tolerant. It is hopeless, broken and uninspiring compared to the "strange" gospel of Christ.

We (David and Wes) believe that we should not look to our culture in order to find out what is normal. Instead, we ought to consider what God says is normal. Therefore, as Christians, we must look to what the Scriptures have to say. When we read Acts 2:42-47, we see what is normal for God's people:

> They devoted themselves to the apostles' teaching and to fellowship, to the breaking of bread and to prayer. Everyone was filled with awe at the many wonders and signs performed by the apostles. All the believers were together and had everything in common. They sold property and possessions to give to anyone who had need. Every day they continued to meet together in the temple courts. They broke bread in their homes and ate together with glad and sincere hearts, praising God and enjoying the favor of all the people. And the Lord added to their number daily those who were being saved (*TNIV*).

In the Early Church, there appeared to be no specific day of the week on which to worship God. Every day was a day to worship God and enjoy His presence. This is how it was in the earliest days of Christianity! Wanting to worship God every day was not strange!

Let's get back to our roots and worship God seven days a week, instead of just on Sunday. The stranger we look to the world, the more normal we look to God. Let's become strange together and call it normal—and not care how the world defines it. Let's challenge our fellow Christians who are just going through the motions to quit trying to fit in with the world's broken ideas. Let's have a strange revolution that becomes a normal way of life. Let's be strange together and, in doing so, bring the Church back to the normalcy God intended for us!

43

CALLED TO BE PECULIAR

JANE ALBRIGHT
Head Women's Basketball Coach, University of Nevada, Reno

*A genuine Christian should be a walking mystery because
he or she is a walking miracle.*
A. W. TOZER

I have been an NCAA Division I women's basketball coach for 30 years. During all of those years, I have been employed at state institutions. Athletics, young people, state universities and Christianity don't always mix well. But I have discovered, as our friend A. W. Tozer wrote, that I can be a walking mystery to those around me. I never proclaim my faith to my athletes in words unless I am asked; however, I can always model how I believe Jesus would live.

The *King James Bible* gives me my identity in 1 Peter 2:9: "But ye are a chosen generation, a royal priesthood, an holy nation, a *peculiar* people; that ye should shew forth the praises of him who hath called you out of darkness into his marvellous light" (emphasis added). Isn't being peculiar the same as being a walking mystery? To me, that is living the life of Christ. In my profession, it has meant that I can actually lose a huge ballgame and walk away with a smile on my face. I can apologize to one of my players when I have wronged her. I can take a Sabbath each week and rarely practice on

Sundays. I can value each of my players and care for her in a loving way. When the press persecutes me because of my beliefs, I can pray for them. When I have been fired because my teams weren't good enough, I could actually be at peace, knowing that my God is in charge of my life and that He will provide and care for me.

Some folks call that walking the walk, not just talking the talk. As Tozer described, my ability to react in these ways, and not in the way of this competitive world, makes me a walking miracle. The mystery, miracle and peculiarity are possible because we have been created to live in an interactive relationship with the Trinity. Anything less than this makes our lives worldly. Often I watch the stress on the faces of non-Christian coaches and wonder what makes them try so hard to win. When they are motivated by money, power, success and prestige, it is the world at its best (or worst). Watching someone strive for more and better and the top is truly NOT a mystery; that is a very predictable path to follow.

When we engage in our work as apprentices of Jesus, we are able to carry on and be in this world, but not of this world. I believe that no matter what your profession is, the life that Christ models teaches us to rest in His provision and care. I encourage you to pursue the life of Christ! He will make you a walking mystery.

44

GOD'S WAY

ESTHER LOVEJOY
Writer

*God promises to hear your prayers, but not to unconditionally
answer them the way you want them answered.*
A. W. TOZER

We all like happy endings—especially happy prayer endings. We
love the story of the widowed woman burning her last piece of coal
just as someone comes through the storm with a load of coal and
food for her family. We love to read how George Mueller sat his
orphans down to give thanks for a meal that didn't exist, and food
arrived before the prayer was over. I even have my own "happy end-
ing" prayer stories—actually lots of them—and they are exciting
and precious to me each time I retell them.

But what about the prayers of faith that don't seem to have
happy endings? What about the times, as Tozer acknowledges in
the above quote, when God hears but doesn't answer the way we
want or expect?

In a few simple words, Tozer states a truth that has been the
basis for much scholarly discussion in theological circles about
the sovereignty of God versus the free will of man. The struggle is
in trying to come up with answers that explain the mysterious. At

some point, this truth becomes for most Christians the source of personal struggle and confusion rather than some esoteric theological debate. Tozer's words represent a dichotomy that, when played out in our own personal circumstances, often leaves us baffled by the ways of God.

Scripture gives us help for such times. Isaiah reminds us that God's ways aren't our ways (see Isaiah 55:8). That alone is a good reminder, but the encouragement comes when we are assured that God's ways aren't just different from ours; they're higher, or superior, to ours. Psalm 18:30 adds more emphasis to this truth by stating that God's ways are perfect. In other words, we can't improve on God's ways or God's answers.

My oldest daughter was born with a minor problem with her left leg. While there was no immediate risk to her overall well-being, there was the potential for more serious problems later in her life. The doctor recommended that we take advantage of the softness and flexibility of her newborn bones and work immediately to straighten them. We trusted his judgment and agreed to do whatever was necessary to bring that little leg around straight.

The decision was easy—the reality of what that involved was much harder. A couple of times each day I took Debbie's little foot and gently turned it until she cried—until we both cried. My only motive was love. My only concern was her best. I would look down at that precious little girl and know that she couldn't possibly understand what was in my heart. She could only feel what came from my hands. Had Debbie been able to articulate a prayer to me then, it probably would have been: "Dear Mommy, please don't twist my foot anymore." But I knew what was best for her and I loved her, so my answer would not have been what she wanted.

"So why pray?" That was a question I was asked by a friend of mine recently. "Why pray," she continued, "if God ultimately does what He wants? Why not just say, 'You know best. Your will be done,' if that's what He's going to do anyhow?"

Not an easy question, but one that has probably been asked by most of us at one time or another. We pray, we trust the Lord, but then God's answer is not what we asked for. If He knows best and chooses best, why bother to pray?

I don't pretend to have all the answers, but I want to share with you where my soul finds rest with this question. If Christianity were just a religion, we would expect it to "work" a certain way and to follow certain rules. But our faith is a personal relationship with the living God, and prayer is a vital part of that relationship. A similar personal relationship exists between us and our children. We want them to come to us and share their hearts. We want them to ask us for what they want, but we also want them to trust our choices and our love. How often have we said no to our children because we knew that what they asked for wasn't good for them or because we had something better planned? As tempting as the desire may be, would we really want our children to walk around saying to us, "You know best. Your will be done"?

God loves us enough to allow us the freedom to ask, and He asks us to love Him enough to trust Him for the answers—even when they aren't what we want or expect. If our foot is being twisted, it is always by a loving hand.

I have often thought of how confused the nation of Israel must have been by God's "failure" to immediately free them from Egypt. Time after time it looked as if God had not answered their prayers. In fact, not only did they not get the answer they wanted, but also things went from bad to worse. Once again they would pray and hope, and once again it would appear as if God were either uncaring or powerless.

But we know the end of the story. God's timing was perfect, and when the Israelites left Egypt, they took with them the plunder of the country. What appeared to be unanswered prayer became the source of great riches for them. And so it can be for us.

Years ago I was privileged to hear Dr. Tozer preach. (I was 12 at the time, so I wasn't aware that it was a privilege.) But all these years later I can clearly remember what he talked about: the will of God. I remember being struck, even at that young age, with the fact that this man loved God deeply and wanted nothing apart from God's will. Tozer's own words give us a wonderful sense of peace in regard to the dilemma of prayers that are answered with seeming indifference: "Outside the will of God, there's nothing I want; and in the will of God, there's nothing I fear."

Tozer was able to state the truth that God always hears our prayers, but He doesn't always answer them according to "our will." Tozer understood this and accepted it with a quiet heart because he was content with God's answer—no matter what it was. And that's a wonderful place to find rest.

> Dear Lord, Your hand has moved in ways I just don't
> understand,
> And I can't find a reason for the sorrow that You send;
> But, Lord, Your Word reminds me that now I know
> in part,
> Until the day I know in full, Lord, let me trust Your heart.

45

TURNING BACK TO GOD

JAMES MEAD
Guitarist, Kutless

I want deliberately to encourage this mighty longing after God.
The lack of it has brought us to our present low estate.
A. W. TOZER

Christian, are you weak and dry? Come to the fountain. Are you perplexed? Do you feel as if you are surrounded on all sides? The Bible says, "We are hard-pressed on every side, yet not crushed; we are perplexed, but not in despair; persecuted, but not forsaken; struck down, but not destroyed" (2 Corinthians 4:8-9). I believe when earthly burdens threaten to overwhelm us, it is because we have attempted to push God out of the way. Let us instead remind ourselves that Jesus is "THE way" (John 14:6, emphasis added)!

What do we gain from the "mighty longing after God" that Tozer wanted us to have? Our lives begin to reflect godliness—from the expectancy of His return to the way we lead our homes, from our faith becoming good works to our attitudes towards our neighbors. A mighty longing after God can be the very first step to our being the love of Christ in action!

It is all too easy to note in what ways our world has fallen into its present low estate as we have turned from God. What is more alarming is the physical effect this turning has on us. King David declared in Psalm 32, "When I kept silent, my bones grew old through my groaning all the day long" (v. 3). We can observe here that there is a noticeable physical effect when we keep silent with the Lord. It goes against His very plan for us! The apostle Paul instructs us to "Rejoice in the Lord always. Again I will say, rejoice!" (Philippians 4:4). We are not to keep silent or disregard the Lord's calling on our lives!

When I do something in life to push God out of the picture, or I attempt to ignore Him, I often feel like I've created a rift between the Lord and me. A few years ago, my wife and I experienced some very tough financial stresses. We had decided to move out of one house and buy a different one. At the same time, the whole housing market began to crash down around everybody. We ended up with no buyers for the house we were trying to sell, and we had two mortgages on our hands for about 9 months. In the meantime, we rented out our old house to help offset our costs. To make a long story short, the renters didn't fulfill their lease terms, and they trashed our house in the short span of three months.

Making matters worse, I was on tour with Kutless a lot during this time. I couldn't be home to help manage this crisis. I must admit that my prayer life during those days was very one-sided. I would basically yell at God, but never try to listen. Emotion was leading my heart. Seeking Him daily became something that was happening less and less as I tried to figure out whom to call—contractors, banks, different real estate agents—about various issues. Finally I called my church and talked to one of our pastors, telling him what dire circumstances my wife and I now found ourselves in. His first step was to lead me to the Lord in prayer. We prayed about having peace in God's assurance that He will never leave us or forsake us (see Hebrews 13:5 and Deuteronomy 31:6). Then he said the church was going to help us.

Shortly after that, we had a new real estate agent and a buyer lined up for our house. However, startling news came from the bank at this point: We were going to have to pay for the closing costs and the difference between the offer and what was still owed on our loan—for a grand total of $21,000! Before I could even start hyperventilating, our pastor called us so we could pray about it together. We decided, after praying, that we should write a letter to the bank asking for a "short sale" and pray over the letter before we sent it. On a Friday evening, after the buyers had already had to move out of their house and into ours, with their own loan for the purchase about to close, we got a call from our bank telling us that they had agreed to accept the short sale and forgive the full $21,000.

In my low state during that trial, I was ignoring God and trying to fix everything myself. I could have been spared so much stress and fear if I had just allowed my heavenly Father to give me peace. I could have been rejoicing that God was going to help me "run the race." The best way that we can have a fervent desire to pursue God is to rejoice in all things. Again, Paul tells us in 1 Thessalonians 5:16 to "rejoice always"—and I believe he reveals to us in the following verses just how we can do that: "Pray without ceasing," he says. "In everything give thanks; for this is the will of God in Christ Jesus for you" (vv. 17-18).

46

GOD-SIZED FAITH

PAM FARREL

Speaker, Author and Co-author of the Bestselling
Men Are Like Waffles, Women Are Like Spaghetti

*What comes into our minds when we think about God is
the most important thing about us.*
A. W. TOZER

There is nothing more vital—more central—to your own self-confidence than your confidence in God. Henry Blackaby and Claude King agree. In their work entitled *Experiencing God*, they write, "How you live your life is a testimony of what you believe about God."[1] Beth Moore contends, "Who we believe God is greatly affects our eternal destinies, but I'd like to suggest that nothing has a greater effect on the quality of our lives and the fulfillment of our destinies. . . . We're wise to ask ourselves the question, Who do I say God is?"[2]

In my book, *Woman of Confidence: Step Into God's Adventure for Your Life*, I challenge our finite minds: "Show me your God, and I will show you your ability to achieve. Small God—small life. Big God—big opportunities and potential await."[3] I choose to dream God-sized dreams, go on God-sized adventures, and make God-sized plans. Your experience can be God-sized too.

Too many of us, however, have lost the ability to think in God-sized terms because we do not see God for who He really is. J. B. Phillips, in *Your God Is Too Small*, explains the quandary in which many of us find ourselves:

> *We are modeling God upon what we know of man.* That is why it is contended here that what at first sight appears to be almost a super-adequate idea of God is, in reality, inadequate— it is based on too tiny a foundation. Man may be made in the image of God; but it is not sufficient to conceive God as nothing more than an infinitely magnified man.[4]

Seeing God as merely an elevated form of ourselves sets us up for failure. We miss out on all God has for us because we fail to see Him as the all-powerful, all-knowing, all-loving God who provides for all our needs. But when we realize that God is more than a man—when we examine His unchanging character—we gain confidence in Him and in His love for us. We become convinced that He will work in and through us—and that the end result will be great!

If social scientists were to look at my humble, dysfunctional beginnings—as the daughter of an alcoholic father, I lived in a home filled with domestic violence until my parents fractured their marriage and the hearts of their children—they would likely contend I would be doomed to repeat the unhealthy patterns of my family of origin. But statistics do not define me. God reached down from heaven and introduced Himself to a little girl who, at age eight, was willing to believe Him at His Word. I actually assumed God meant it when He said things like:

> For nothing will be impossible with God (Luke 1:37, *NASB*).

> I am God, and there is no other. . . . I say: My purpose will stand, and I will do all that I please. . . . What I have said, that will I bring about; what I have planned, that will I do (Isaiah 46:9-11, *NIV*).

I decided early on to agree with those who walked with God—like Jeremiah, who said, "Ah, Sovereign LORD, you have made the heavens and the earth by your great power and outstretched arm. Nothing is too hard for you" (Jeremiah 32:17, *NIV*).

These are lofty words—but most days I step out in meager faith and cry out like the grieving father pleading with Jesus: "I do believe; help me overcome my unbelief!" (Mark 9:24, *NIV*). And Jesus answers me, as He did His disciples: "I tell you the truth, if you have faith as small as a mustard seed, you can say to this mountain, 'Move from here to there' and it will move. Nothing will be impossible for you" (Matthew 17:20, *NIV*).

God, in His mercy, is the Father who knows how to give good gifts to His children (see Matthew 7:11; Luke 11:13). God took my little seed of faith and added Himself! I didn't repeat those toxic patterns of my heritage; instead, God created a new legacy. I am happily married to an amazing Christian leader who also overcame a home of chaos by the blood of the Lamb. We have carved out more than 30 happy years together and raised three sons who also love, serve and BELIEVE Jesus. We have penned more than 35 books, and those words have been translated into more than 12 languages. We have traveled to many countries to speak, teach and encourage others to stake a claim in the person of Christ to find hope and help for life and to gain the ability to dream God-sized dreams. We pack up our bags and climb onto planes, week after week, motivated as we embrace God's commands to:

Let the redeemed of the LORD tell their story (Psalm 107:2, *TNIV*).

Give praise to the LORD, call on his name; make known among the nations what he has done (Psalm 105:1, *TNIV*).

There are two ways to live life: by fear or by faith. My friend Jill Savage, founder of *Hearts at Home*, when overwhelmed, says, "Don't look at the mountain; look at the mountain mover." So on those days when I feel faint of heart, when the world feels like it is caving in on me, and when I want to stay in bed and pull the covers over my head, instead I choose faith—the powerful, protecting, providing faith that comes when you abide in Christ. Jesus said:

> I am the vine, you are the branches; he who abides in Me and I in him, he bears much fruit, for apart from Me you can do nothing.... If you abide in Me, and My words abide in you, ask whatever you wish, and it will be done for you (John 15:5,7, *NASB*).

I once heard that "abide" means to remain or stay as if pitching a tent. My faith isn't something I conjure up; it is simply the act of driving in a peg of trust, and pressing up the meager tarp of my will. I choose, decide and opt for camping out in the person of God. "The name of the LORD is a strong tower; the righteous runs into it and is safe" (Proverbs 18:10, *NASB*).

My teen son, one day, gave me a cherished compliment that I have accepted as my life's creed: "Mom, you have crazy faith!" Call me crazy, but I think the most sane alternative, the "safest" choice, and the most exciting, adventure-expanding option is to daily pitch my tent into, hang my heart on, dig my heels in, and park myself on the truth—*God IS who He says He is.*

I am redeemed. I say so. So does Tozer—and so can you.

Notes

1. Henry T. Blackaby and Claude V. King, *Experiencing God* (Nashville, TN: Lifeway, 1990), p. 109.

2. Beth Moore, *A Taste of Believing God* (Nashville, TN: Lifeway, 2008) pp. 10,13.

3. Pam Farrel, *Woman of Confidence: Step Into God's Adventure for Your Life* (Eugene, OR: Harvest House, 2009), p. 27.

4. J. B. Phillips, *Your God Is Too Small* (New York: Collier, 1961), p. 42.

47

THE SWEET WILL
OF GOD

TONY NOLAN
Tour Pastor, Casting Crowns Lifesong Tour and Winter Jam

*I am Thy servant to do Thy will, and that will is
sweeter to me than position or riches or fame, and I choose it
above all things on Earth or in Heaven.*
A. W. TOZER

I want to start with a moment of personal confession: I am totally into sweets! My favorite has to be butter pecan ice cream. No, it's M&Ms. No, it must be Oreos. No, it's . . . You get the point. I love sweets, and I could eat all of them forever!

As I sit here watching some hummingbirds fight over the succulent sugar in my feeder, I'm thinking we may be kin. These guys are fully crazy about the stuff in the feeder. They dart back and forth at each other, fighting over who will get the next chance to siphon out the clear yummy gold. Their affinity for sweets is undeniable.

The psalmist said he had that kind of addiction to God's Word. He said God's Word was sweeter to him than honey—or the whole honeycomb for that matter. Here is how he put it in Psalm 19:9-11: "The fear of the LORD is clean, enduring forever; the judgments of the LORD are true and righteous altogether. More to be desired are they than gold, yea, than much fine gold; sweeter also than honey and the honeycomb. Moreover by them Your servant is warned, and in keeping them there is great reward." How cool is that? The most amazing thing is that he wasn't talking about the promises or the blessings of God, which I really dig, but the judgments of God. Did you see that? He is saying God's Word is so sweet to him that he even loves to drink up the judgments! WOW! How did this kind of affection develop in the psalmist's heart? I am no expert. My name is Tony, and I am just a guy. But I can make an observation. The person who said this "sweeter than honey" thing was a song dude. David loved writing and singing songs. His writings take up the pages of the longest book in the Bible: Psalms. There has to be a connection. I think it is this: What your heart sings about, it brings about. I have found this to be true in my life. When I fill my heart with songs about God's will, it makes me long for God's will. I crave it more than sugar! Tozer said that God's will was "sweeter" to him than anything else on earth. He also was a man of worship. He had a passion for worship that was based on God's Word, and that passion proved to be a factor in creating a craving for the sweet will of God for his life.

PRIORITIZING PRAYER

ADAM AGEE
Lead Singer, Stellar Kart

The key to prayer is simply praying.
A. W. TOZER

My life is full. It's full of family, friends, work, play and other random activities that consume my waking hours and follow me mercilessly into my abbreviated slumber. The rhythm of my life moves at such a fast tempo that I have to make a conscious effort to slow down and budget my time to avoid burning out like a cheap cigarette in the hand of a crooner. I internally justify my hectic schedule because, at the core, I honestly do hope my efforts are spent helping others and at the same time increasing the quality of life for my family. This justification leads to the incorrect reorganization of priorities, with prayer finding its place near the bottom of the time consumption hierarchy. Prayer is an action I never regret, and one I think *about* often—so why is it so hard to find time to pray? Let's just say life is . . . busy.

Because time is such a precious and fleeting commodity, I thrive on finding the simplest and quickest solution to any situation that arises. I love to unravel mysteries and discover meanings behind the meanings of things. I feel the need to understand the "why" behind music, clichés, traditions and other facets of life to which most of us don't give a second thought. But some explanations elude me. Unraveling the mystery of prayer is one of those impossible endeavors. Not only is the task "above my pay grade," but it would also take a lifetime just to scratch the surface of understanding how and why prayer is even possible.

Prayer is a complex supernatural phenomenon that offers no scientific explanation or evidence around which we can wrap our limited human minds. How do I explain to somebody that I am conversing casually with the same God who created the very air I'm breathing? At the same time, prayer is amazingly simple. The most basic acts of sentient beings are observations and thoughts. We don't even have to verbalize our thoughts to communicate with our Creator. He has made communication with Him so easy that we really have no excuse to not "pray without ceasing" (1 Thessalonians 5:17). How could I possibly not have enough time to talk to the One to whom I owe my very existence and reason for living? Unfortunately, it happens all too frequently in my life.

I desperately want to know more about the character of God and to understand His plans, but so many life distractions get in the way of that pursuit. Perhaps you find yourself in the same situation. Maybe you wish your prayer life were more consistent and vibrant than it is. Maybe you have the best intentions about devoting time to communion with God through prayer, but one urgent matter after another draws you in other directions.

Or possibly, in our culture saturated with ever-accessible information and countless "how-to" resources, you feel that if you just knew more about prayer, you would be able to do it better. If you read one more book, attended one more seminar or found the perfect prayer group in your community, you would then be equipped and ready to pray as you feel you ought.

But here is what I am discovering—and what I think Tozer longed for us to understand: Learning to pray is not only about understanding and comprehension, but also—and more so— about practice and execution. All the knowledge I can glean from this world pales in comparison to the revelation God gives through direct communication with Him. Ultimately, I control the way I choose to spend my time. If, as Tozer claims, "the key to prayer is simply praying," then we have found our solution. We must simply pray.

THE "HIGHLY-SOUGHT" GOSPEL THAT DOESN'T EXIST

ALEX MCFARLAND
Co-Host, *SoundRezn* Radio Show; Religion and Culture Expert

How utterly terrible is the current idea that Christians can serve God at their own convenience.

A. W. TOZER

How would the level of twenty-first century American discipleship measure up if compared "toe to toe" with Tozer? The quotation above indicates how Tozer would react to the lack of obedience that characterizes much of the Church today. Here was a man who wore many hats in his service to God: He was a pastor, church planter, missions pioneer, author, and more. Selective obedience to the clear dictates of Scripture is something that would have been completely foreign to A. W. Tozer.

What would Tozer say to a generation of evangelicals described by a *Newsweek* magazine article in the following manner: "Today's new Christians tend to take from the Bible whatever fits their needs—and ignore whatever fails to resonate with their own . . . traditions"?[1] I attribute the current state of church health in America to the spread of a "highly-sought gospel that doesn't exist." Let me explain what I mean. Of course, the historic Christian message (that Jesus died and arose in payment for our sins)—this gospel certainly *does* exist, and it is true and relevant for all people. But a less-than-biblical "gospel" has infected our culture. It minimizes God's claim on our lives and ignores our responsibility to surrender all to Him.

Through the corridors of time, Tozer's voice rings out with convicting honesty: "How utterly terrible is the current idea that Christians can serve God at their own convenience." Were he with us today, I believe Tozer would agree with fundamental truths such as the following:

There cannot be true redemption without righteousness. Let's face it: Some people want forgiveness of sin without a change in lifestyle. They want Jesus' love without Jesus' lordship. If Jesus has come into your life, your behavior should be characterized by righteousness. If this is not the case, personal inventory in the spirit of 2 Corinthians 13:5 might be in order: "Examine yourselves to see whether you are in the faith; test yourselves" (*NIV*).

There is no absolute truth without personal application. It is not enough to acknowledge that truth and universal moral absolutes exist. The crux of the matter is this: What is our response to the light we've been given? With revelation and understanding comes the responsibility to amend our lives in light of that revelation.

There is no such thing as a Bible without boundaries. Having spoken personally with hundreds of professed atheists, former church members and skeptics, I have come to believe that the default position of humans is to try to circumvent what the Bible has to say about sin. One strategy is to assert that certain behaviors, identified as sin in the Bible, have been rendered acceptable by changes in cultural context. However, as far as I can tell, no past sins have now been "de-classified." The Bible has a lot to say about our freedom in Christ, but it also speaks forcefully about God's standards and moral boundaries.

There are no privileges without responsibility. Could it be that as the flesh struggles to dominate the spirit (see Romans 7:7–8:17), we desire the riches of *sonship* without the *responsibility* of discipleship? Our wonderful reformation doctrine of the "priesthood of the believer" is increasingly used as a justification for what I call "militant autonomy." Is the born-again person set free in Christ? Absolutely. But this is all the more reason to set high standards for our life and conduct.

There is no evangelism without involvement. We all want to see people reached for Christ, but do we desire this enough to "get in the game"? Each Christian is to be a representative of the gospel. We cannot expect "somebody else" to witness to the lost neighbor or unbelieving coworker.

There is no spiritual fruit without tangible investment. It has been said that a person's wallet is usually the last thing to get converted. Real spiritual change is possible for our nation and world, but it will come about only through the investment of God's people. I am not speaking only in terms of finances, though that is one way we are to participate in God's work. There must also be investment of *ourselves*—of our time, abilities and influence.

There is no heavenly hope without earthly preparation. I am convinced that great numbers of Americans are headed for a rude awakening on the day they stand before Jesus Christ. They may have recited the "sinner's prayer" or walked an aisle to "make a spiritual decision," yet they have never experienced a changed life. The one who hopes to stand before the Lord in confidence and joy *someday* had better bow before the Lord in repentance and obedience *this day*.

There is an old saying: "We know what we like, and we like what we know." It can be hard to change long-held habits or to admit that we've been wrong about something. Perhaps you've heard the account of how Albert Einstein reacted to the conclusions implied by his general theory of relativity. The year was 1917, and Einstein wasn't completely comfortable with all that he was discovering—especially the unavoidable conclusion that the universe had a beginning. The universe, it turned out, was not eternal, as Einstein had believed it was.

Of course, this meant that something outside the universe had brought it into existence. Einstein was so unhappy about this reality that he intentionally changed the terms of his equation to artificially allow for an eternal universe. The so-called "fudge factor"

Einstein smuggled in required division by zero (a commonly recognized mathematical error). The scientist's personal bias, rather than the evidence, shaped his conclusions. Einstein called his "fudge factor" the "greatest blunder of my career."

If we're honest with ourselves and honest before God, we smuggle spiritual "fudge factors" into our lives. First Corinthians 6:19-20 says that our lives are not our own—we belong completely to God. Yet we justify disobedience to the Lord by telling ourselves that we are "free in Christ." In Luke 6:46, Jesus poses the question, "Why do you call me 'Lord, Lord' and do not do what I say?" (NIV). Good question. The fact is that if Jesus had the place in our lives that He deserves, our personal lives and our world would look a lot different.

Tozer lamented a Church that serves God selectively, at Christians' "own convenience." May the Holy Spirit so move in our lives that that "current idea" will become a past memory.

Note

1. Kenneth L. Woodward, "The Changing Face of the Church," *Newsweek*, April 15, 2001. http://www.thedailybeast.com/newsweek/2001/04/15/the-changing-face-of-the-church.html.

ENJOYED BY GOD

MARK FOREMAN
Senior Pastor, North Coast Calvary Chapel, Carlsbad, California

*God is going to be as pleased to have you with Him in heaven as
you will be to be there with Him.*
A. W. TOZER

Our headlights parted the black night as we silently climbed the
long, steep, winding road to our mountain cabin in Twin Peaks.
Disturbed by a conversation with a friend, I was battling tears, and
my wife knew that silence was my friend. Arriving home exhausted,
I managed to build a fire. I curled up with a blanket and sat listening to the crackling fire while pondering my friend's words: "God
thinks about us and loves us in detailed ways. Clearly loving us at
the cross, He loves us, thinks about us and wants to be with us."

Was this true? Could the infinite, eternal God love me in the
minutia of my life? Am I truly precious to Him in a personal way,
or was this simply modern humanism bleeding over into Christianity? Was the cross Christ's primary act of love for faceless humanity, or was it His great loving act, with thousands of other
loving thoughts and actions clustered around it? God's love
seemed bigger than life, and this idea was striking me at my core.

Growing up, I had been driven by performance. I was the quiet,
often unnoticed middle child. Wanting my parents' and society's

attention and approval, I learned to perform—and it worked. I performed for grades, musical attention and trophies in sports. I was the best I could be when I was on the world's stage. It was then that I was noticed, and my parents would brag to their friends about me.

Becoming a believer as a young adult, I transferred this same performance-based relationship to God. Just as I had always performed for my dad, wanting his approval, I now also performed for my heavenly Father. Of course, I knew clearly that I could not earn my salvation. That was a gift. I knew I was saved by grace through faith alone. Still, to be noticed or loved in my daily life, I performed for God and others.

As a pastor, I did the same. I taught Bible studies, led worship, organized and planted churches, and spoke at conferences—enjoying the attention these duties brought to my soul. The stage had shifted, but it was still a stage, and I hoped that God would value me.

My expectation of heaven was no better. How could a God with millions of middle children ever notice my arrival? There were too many other important people to greet. It would take ten thousand millennia for God even to discover I was there.

I stared at the fire, feeling lonely and abandoned. I had always taught others that God "accepts us just the way we are." But to me, acceptance meant "to tolerate." I was well aware of the doctrine of justification and its legal implications: I was forgiven. But that didn't mean God was excited to be with me. To me it simply meant that God put up with me.

Then, out of the silence, God spoke three words that cut through my flowing tears. They were not words I could have made up, nor were they obscured by any excess verbiage. God didn't waste one syllable. Just three words, pregnant with meaning: "I enjoy you."

Could that be? Was that God's word to me—that He was pleased with me and wanted to be with me without performance? That He didn't just accept me, but actually longed for me, wanted me and would be pleased to have me in heaven? Zephaniah 3:17 declares:

The LORD your God is with you,
   he is mighty to save.
He will take great delight in you,
   he will quiet you with his love,
he will *rejoice* over you with *singing* (*NIV*, emphasis added).

I sobbed, realizing that my Father not only judicially forgave me along with the rest of humanity but also personally loved, wanted and enjoyed me. I was a delight to him. My salvation was a personal redemption, not simply a corporate, legal act of history. Just as Boaz in the book of Ruth wanted to personally redeem Ruth so that she could be his beloved wife, so too Jesus personally sought me out for an eternal, loving relationship with Him.

Tozer once penned, "God is going to be as pleased to have you with Him in heaven as you will be to be there with Him." I guess it's true. I don't have to perform or try to earn His love. I am not just a number among the millions who will be in heaven. I won't get lost in the crowd. He knows me and will come looking for me upon my arrival.

Meanwhile, He enjoys me now and is pleased to have me as His child. Like the best of parents, He wants to be with me and invest His nature into me. He enjoys watching me use my gifts and talents for His pleasure. His eyes smile as I take my little steps of obedience toward Him. He enjoys me and I enjoy Him.

TENDING THE ETERNAL FLAME

ALYSSA BARLOW
Singer and Keyboardist, BarlowGirl

If my fire is not large it is yet real, and there may be those who can light their candle at its flame.
A. W. TOZER

Recently, my sisters and I took some much-needed time off. We decided to use up our nine-year collection of airline miles and finally take our dream trip to Italy. Our first stop was Rome. I was so looking forward to seeing the history and art I had only read about. As we walked through ancient Rome, we came to a place that will stay with me forever. The grounds were brilliant green, with pools lining the middle, and all along the sides were tall white statues of Roman women in beautiful dresses.

As we walked in further, I began to feel a peace I had not felt anywhere else that day. Our tour guide began to describe the place we were standing in as the home of the women who were known as the "Vestal Virgins." These women were the most honored of all women in their day; they had more privileges than their peers and were held in the highest respect. However, these women had also made a great sacrifice.

In those days, the emperor required a fire to be kept lit continually—day and night—so that in the evening all the people of the surrounding villages could come and take some of the fire back to their homes. This fire was never to go out, and the Vestals were the ones chosen to keep the flame lit. They each sacrificed 30 years of their lives to this task. Training for the position lasted 10 years, then 10 years were spent as a Vestal, and the final 10 were devoted to raising up the next generation who would carry on their work. They were each also required to take a vow of purity—to remain completely set apart for the position they held.

As I listened to this, my heart began to beat a bit faster, which always tends to happen when I'm hearing stories of those who lived lives for more than themselves. It came to me in a flash: *That is why I live! To keep the fire lit so that others around me can in turn light their candles at my flame!* Yes, it has been a sacrifice. In fact, I can say that as well as being the greatest honor of my life, this "fire-tending" has also been the hardest thing I've ever done.

Just to clarify, I'm not referring to my calling as a musician. That is simply a visual overflow of the fire that my family and I have been keeping in our personal lives for years—the hours spent, while no one is looking, dedicated to one thing. Many times during the past few years, I've questioned my motives: *Do I tend the fire for the audience, or would I still do it if I weren't on stage every night? Do I do it to enhance the concert, or am I really, truly this passionate about God?*

Those questions, when I got brutally honest with myself, left me painfully aware of my own need to enter the King's palace and once again light my candle at His flame—not so I could go out and be "Alyssa Barlow the performer," but just so I could be "Alyssa Barlow the daughter." God's not looking for great men and women; He is just looking for those willing to prove the greatness of their God. He is looking for Davids, Daniels and Esthers—normal men and women who had passionate relationships with God before anyone knew who they were. Their fire was never for show; it was so high on their list of priorities that they were more than willing to lay down their own lives to protect it.

In my personal search for this truth, I have found one thing: If I never step in front of an audience again—if I never have another chance to yell into the microphone my passion for God—I still have a strong desire to keep my fire burning. One of my favorite lyrics, by a band called Switchfoot, truly sums up what I feel: "I'm on fire when you're near me, I'm on fire when you speak, I'm on fire burning at these mysteries."[1]

I keep a fire lit because when I'm near Him, something in me comes alive. My walk is different, my words change, and my thoughts toward people get refined. Then suddenly I realize that everywhere I go, I am affecting others with my ongoing fire. It's no longer a "Sunday morning thing." It's an all day, every day, sub-conscious effort to see and serve those who are cold and need some warming up. It is an all day, every day conscious decision to stay close to His fire, no matter what it costs me—and let me tell you, it has cost me my life. However, "life" is a very relative term when compared to all I've gained. I have chosen to give my life to tend a fire that was never meant to go out.

Note

1. Switchfoot, "On Fire," from the album *The Beautiful Letdown* (New York: Sony Music Entertainment, Inc., 2003).

Deadly Work

Kimberly L. Smith
Author, *Passport Through Darkness;* President, Make Way Partners

There must be a work of God in destruction before we are free.
We must invite the cross to do its deadly work within us.
A. W. TOZER

The week after I agreed to write a reflection on this quote, I found myself drunk. That is not a metaphor.

Jesus said we are fishers of men. But the gnarled thread of sexual abuse has twisted through my life from childhood to middle age so many times that I often feel it has knotted my soul into a useless tangle of fishing line. What good thing can the snag of me possibly catch?

Cast into the troubled sea of life, I swim day and night—hoping the burning salt in my wounds will clean and heal them. I dangle wildly in the tossing waves—longing to be a lure some lost soul can latch onto. Instead, the whale of brokenness swallows me up. My brokenness. My husband's brokenness. My children's brokenness. My parents' brokenness. And the overwhelming sum of brokenness—the ridiculous, violent, insane, absolute evil preying upon the orphans of our tragically fallen world.

Invite the cross to do its deadly work within?

Merely reading those letters as they scrawl across my screen, forming their bloodthirsty nails of words, fills me with fear and anguish. Given the unbearable brutality of this world, sometimes it seems safer to crawl inside a bottle than cling to a brokenhearted prayer. But I won't. Not today, anyway.

Instead, today, I ask myself to consider what it means to invite the deadly work of the cross into my life, specifically into my disease of alcoholism.

Every day, the cross cries out to each of us—longing to violently plunge into the depths of our iniquitous lives of self-centeredness, gluttony, pornography, bitterness, blame or playing make-believe-church—where our good works intoxicate us and mask our image-driven motives and insatiable hunger to control.

But today, in this moment, the blood of the cross drips the letters of my name, and the examined life begs me—K-i-m-b-e-r-l-y L. S-m-i-t-h—to invite the deadly work of the cross into the menagerie of me where I face the rabid beast of alcoholism. There. I've said it, written it. Finally, out loud, in public, and with bloodstained ink.

There's no turning back now. I set my face like a flint.

My Golgotha, or place of the skull, is where my head stops its frenetic work to pre-configure all the answers. What comes next? What do people expect of me? How will I handle their reactions to my endless failures? What will image-driven Christians do with my disquieting honesty? Will they, or even I, ever see my story the way Jesus does?

The brutality of all my disappointment, anger, fear, sin, loss and helpless impotence drives me onto the gouging grain of the cross. As the finger-size splinters dig deep into the spine of my soul, I writhe—looking for another way. *"My Father, if it is possible, let this cup pass from Me"* (Matthew 26:39).

My fists open. Again, they make way for the bloody work of the cross. The first nails pound into the palms of my control and shame. Hammers forge the clubbed feet of my fear and doubt into the long lower beam.

My spirit twists and thrashes. My flesh begs for escape, demanding its right to fight and defend. Yet, I am bound to my cross.

It is doing its deadly work on me . . . God help me . . . in me.

Mocking encircles me—like the wild cackle from murderous packs of laughing hyenas I've heard in the dead of too many nights as they fed upon helpless Darfur orphans.

A swoosh of air catches my breath as the sudden pull of ropes catapults me high into the air. With a swift jerk I am up, my head banging its thorny crown into the back of the cross.

Gravity tears at my flesh, sending splashes of blood from my every gaping wound. In the midst of the jeering mockers, my Irish and Cherokee grandfathers stand as a great cloud of witnesses, weeping for the curse they passed on to me.

Their cries rise to me, a bitter hyssop soaked in some strange mingling of their tears and my blood. I cannot swallow it. Instead, I cry out to my Father. *"Where are You? Why aren't You here? My God, My God, I am so alone!"*

The eternity of a time, and times, and half a time, passes before my skewered body is lowered. Will this sudden fall break the fragile reed of my body? Will the forces of darkness break my legs?

Not a bone is broken. Instead the sharp spear of death is finally plunged through my side. I welcome it and succumb to its glory. I need fear it no longer, for passing through this darkness is my last hope. "Lord, I believe; help my unbelief!" (Mark 9:24).

Finally. Absolute surrender in the one place my broken humanity can know it . . . in the tomb.

Utter silence.

Complete peace.

Free of all struggle, abuse, strife, worry, shame and resistance. Death finally does its bidding on me, devouring the smallness of my belief. Dismantling the intellectual knowledge to which I have clung. Obliterating the image of my life I'd worked so hard to create. Wolfing down my fear of what I might become.

In this darkness, from this nothingness, seeds of splendor sprout. The cave of me rumbles with the surge of new life. In the preening dawn, Splendor speaks new life into my decaying bones.

They snap with hope as I spring from the tomb, no longer believing in a new day, but being one.

This new day—this resurrected heart—can never stray too far from the dark tomb, for this is the only place where God makes each dead piece of me new. I long for the day my Lover—my Groom—returns to me, for me, making the whole of me glorious, shimmering with His radiance.

In the meantime, I drag my limping faith up the brutal, sober hill of Golgotha . . . facing down the fear that the dangerous snag of me can lure and catch nothing good for Him. The tattered basket of me holds not even five loaves and two fishes.

So here, desperately clinging to the freedom of the unfurled sail of God on the stormy sea of life, I howl above the crashing waves, "Here I am. Slay me first, then send me out."

Love, from a place very near Golgotha, your sister along the journey,

So also the chief priests, with the scribes and elders, mocked him,
saying, "He saved others; he cannot save himself."
MATTHEW 27:41-42, *ESV*

53

FREEDOM
FROM STUFF

SHANE CLAIBORNE

Speaker, Advocate and Author of *The Irresistible Revolution*

As long as we imagine we own anything, that thing owns us.
As soon as we know that we own nothing, then God owns us.
A. W. TOZER

Sometimes we find that the more we have, the less we become. The more possessions we own, the more we become possessed by them. As Jesus said, we can gain the whole world and lose our souls (see Matthew 16:26). That may be one of the reasons the wealthiest places on earth have the highest rates of loneliness, depression and suicide. We can end up the richest and loneliest people in the world.

The gifts of God are wonderful and beautiful. Tasty food, warm clothes, a nice piece of art or a good book—these are certainly good things. However, sometimes the best thing to do with the best things in life is give them away. We give money and possessions power over us when we cannot let them go—and we free ourselves and take away their power when we give them away.

We who follow Christ have a peculiar way of thinking of the stuff of earth. We do not put our hope in the stuff here that moths can eat up, rust can destroy, and thieves can steal. I've learned this lesson from homeless folks and neighbors who haven't had a lot of stuff, and who know that what little they have can be taken away at any time—by thieves or by the police, by fires or by the repo man—so they are thankful for every meal, every moment, every day.

A few years ago, we had a bad fire that started in an abandoned factory and then spread into the nearby residential community, burning down a block of our neighborhood. One of my neighbors, whose home was badly damaged, was interviewed after the fire. I'll never forget the answer he gave when the journalist asked him how he was feeling. He confidently said he wasn't worried about anything—that our neighborhood would pull together to take care of one another. Then he winsomely said the funniest thing: "And since the old factory burned to the ground, I can see the moon for the first time from our block, and it is beautiful." That's a different way of looking at the situation. We Christians really do have a peculiar way of thinking about possessions.

I think of the response of one of the young beggars in Calcutta when I got him an ice cream cone. Some friends and I were playing in the street with a bunch of the street kids, and one of them informed me it was his birthday. So I bought him an ice cream cone. His response was brilliant. His first instinct was to share it. It was too good to keep for himself. He yelled to all the other kids, "We've got ice cream." As they ran over, he lined them up, insisting, "Everyone is going to get a lick." He then proceeded down the line, giving each kid a lick—and saving one last big ol' sloppy lick for me.

There was no sense of ownership or entitlement or greed. Just joy.

I think of one of my favorite saints, Brother Juniper. He was one of the brothers of St. Francis in Assisi, Italy, in the thirteenth century—and he was notorious for giving everything away. At one point, he was left in charge of the cathedral. Some folks came in need of money, so he gave them all the treasures from the altar of the cathedral (and got in a little trouble for it!). On another occasion, he had given his clothing away so many times that he got scolded by his superior and ordered not to give his garments away anymore. Immediately after this rebuke by the superior, a half-naked beggar in need of clothing approached Juniper as he walked down the street. Juniper thought for a moment and said, "My dear brother, you have caught me at a bad time. I have been forbidden by my superior to give my clothing away. However, if you try to take it from me, I sure won't stop you."

If we cannot hold our possessions with open hands, then they own us.

Some of the happiest people I know have had very little stuff. A reporter was once talking with Mother Teresa and said naively, "Mother Teresa, I wouldn't do what you do for a million dollars." She shot back, "I wouldn't do it for a million dollars either." She did it because it was what she was made for.

It is said that the early Christians often had hungry people who came to them in need, and if there was not enough food for everyone to eat, then no one would eat. They would fast until there was enough food for all to share. That is a radical economic vision, rooted in love of God and neighbor. It is with this freedom that we can still laugh, even in a recession. For we declare that God is good, no matter what is happening on Wall Street. Our hope is not built on America or militaries or the Dow Jones Industrial Average. "Our hope is built on nothing less than Jesus' blood and righteousness . . . all other ground is sinking sand."

These are just a few stories of saints throughout history—of people who have a strange way of looking at stuff. We trust in the God who led the Hebrew slaves into the wilderness and provided for them. We trust in the God who sent the apostles out with no money, spare clothes or food and provided for them. And we trust in the God who cares for the lilies and the sparrows and invites us to live like them.

They don't own much, but they seem to be pretty content with life—God takes care of them just fine without a 401(k) or savings account. And they are free.

54

THE GIFT OF BEING UNNECESSARY

DAVID CARR
Drummer, Third Day

Teach us, O God, that nothing is necessary to Thee. Were anything neces-
sary to Thee that thing would be the measure of Thine imperfection: and
how could we worship one who is imperfect? If nothing is necessary to
Thee, then no one is necessary, and if no one, then not we. Thou dost seek
us though Thou does not need us. We seek Thee because we need Thee, for
in Thee we live and move and have our being. Amen.

A. W. TOZER

Several years ago, I was set free from the worry and preoccupation
of how God could or would use me. For a long time, I had felt a
nagging sense of incompleteness in me, and there was a strong
urge to "get the show on the road" with regard to my obedience
and service to God. I turned to every possible source for answers to
my quandary: books, sermons, friends, pastors, counseling and
anything else that seemed promising. I hoped that someone or
something would help me jump-start my faith and get it moving
in a real and tangible way.

I was also lugging around a major weight of guilt concerning
my giving—or lack thereof. *Maybe next month I'll really start tithing*
and giving to good causes, I thought again and again. Next month

never seemed to come, and I was sure I could feel God's impatience mounting—like a bill collector making yet another threatening phone call. This burden weighed on me, and I knew (or at least I felt) that the clock was ticking. Someday, either lightning would strike or God would find some clever way to let me have it. It was His money, and He wanted it right away.

Fortunately, the Holy Spirit began to reveal something refreshing and, quite honestly, pretty unexpected.

"Guess what? I don't need you!"

What?

"I have carried out My will up to this point without your help, and I am capable of accomplishing My purposes without you. But because I love you, you are invited to participate in My work. When you do, you will experience life—My life!"

God simply does not need us at all—nor does He need our money. He has plenty of money and is quite able to do whatever He wants to do. From the moment I came to this realization, the pressure was off. I began to see things in a new light as my perspective shifted from one of guilt to a much more hopeful and grace-filled point of view. Besides, I had begun to see that if anything good did come from me, it was only because of the One who was in me. Grace began to take on a whole new meaning. It was grace that caused me to want to be obedient, and grace that built in me the desire to give. Guilt had no place, and the desires became pure.

One of the amazing things about God's grace is its boundlessness. With human beings, the fruit of the Spirit have apparent limits to them, but with an all-perfect God, neither the fruit of His Spirit nor the grace through which they come can be maxed out. He is infinite, as are His abilities to love us, to give us joy and to give us peace. He is perfectly patient and infinitely kind, good and faithful. He is gentle with us, and through the Holy Spirit we are given self-control.

How wonderfully freeing it is not to be needed—especially when we stand in the shadow of Jesus' almighty power, knowing that apart from Him, we can do nothing, yet through Him, we can do all things!

55

PURSUING
GOD'S TOUCH

ELMER TOWNS
Co-Founder, Liberty University
Author, *Fasting for Spiritual Breakthrough*

We should come to church not anticipating entertainment but expecting
the high and holy manifestation of God's presence.
A. W. TOZER

The winds swirled around my Toronto, Ontario, hotel on an early
evening—right around sunset—in the winter of 1961. I had asked
the bellboy how to get to Avenue Road Alliance Church and gave
him the street address.

"It is easy to find, only 30 minutes away." He explained it was
just one bus ride from downtown and then a two-block walk to
the church. I had a choice of riding a van out to People's Church,
where the great pastor, Oswald J. Smith, would be preaching that
evening, or facing a lonely bus ride and walking a few blocks in
threatening weather.

In spite of the less than ideal conditions, I chose Tozer. The
auditorium was not sufficiently lit to warm me up from my chilly
walk, nor was the music powerful enough to stir my emotions.
On the surface, the gathering could be described as an average
Sunday evening service in an average evangelical church anywhere

in Canada. But on a deeper level, there was something different about the music and the service. I felt the presence of God in the auditorium.

I did not know what to expect in the way of a sermon; I had never heard Tozer preach, and no one told me what to expect. I did not know whether I would find his teaching rousing, or deeply meditative, or practical.

As a young man, I had determined to hear as many great preachers of my day as possible. Today, I still have their names listed in the front of my old *Scofield Bible*: Lewis Sperry Chafer, J. Sidlow Baxter, Peter Marshall, Billy Sunday, Kenneth Wuest, J. Oliver Buswell and Dawson Trotman—just to name a few. Mine was not hero worship, nor did I want to sit under their sermons to learn something new or titillating. Since these great men knew God, walked with God, and had the influence of God on their ministries, I wanted their God to touch me. That is why I went to hear A. W. Tozer. I wanted to touch God, but more importantly, I wanted God to touch me.

To tell you the truth, I don't remember the title of his message or its content. I don't even remember the passage of Scripture he taught from, and I did not write down anything for future reference. But I do remember experiencing the presence of God in the building. I remember feeling that Tozer knew God in a way that I didn't. In spite of not remembering what he said that evening, I will forever be glad I braved the wind and rain to hear A. W. Tozer preach that evening. Being in the presence of this godly man strengthened my own longing for God.

In the end, this was the value of hearing these faithful men of God preach. It wasn't about the particular words they spoke from the pulpit. It was about the inspiration and challenge their examples provided. I will never forget sitting in a room with A. W. Tozer and wanting to be like him—and to know his God as he knew Him.

56

COMPLETING OUR ASSIGNMENT

BISHOP KENNETH C. ULMER

Senior Pastor-Teacher, Faithful Central Bible Church,
Inglewood, California

Only a disciple can make a disciple.
A. W. TOZER

Jesus is on His way to Calvary. In this last meeting before the cross, He prays for His disciples and all believers in what has come to be known as the High Priestly Prayer. In Jesus' words to His Father, there is an interesting revelation. He prays, "Father . . . I have brought you glory on earth by completing the work you gave me to do" (John 17:1,4, *NIV*). Glorifying God is in the vocabulary—and among the activities—of most Christians. We sing about giving glory to God, we pray for the glory of God and we strive to glorify the Lord. But how do you do it? How do you glorify the Lord? How do you give and bring glory to God? Jesus gives us insight into glorifying God in His prayer.

First of all, whatever it means to glorify God—we can know that Jesus did it! He clearly says, "I have brought you glory." He then goes on to reveal how He did it. He says He did it "by completing the work you gave me to do." Ah. There is a clue. According to Jesus, at least one of the ways we bring glory to God—glorify God—is by completing the work He gives us to do. The phrase describing what Jesus did carries the idea of completing and accomplishing a work, task or assignment given. The Father had given Him an assignment, and Jesus did it. Eugene Peterson, in his marvelous contemporary paraphrase of this passage, says Jesus prayed, "I glorified you on earth by completing down to the last detail what you assigned me to do" (John 17:4, *THE MESSAGE*). There it is: According to Jesus, we glorify God by completing our God-given assignments in life. Of course, the next logical question is: What is our assignment? What assignment did Jesus give us believers? Well, let's stay with the story.

Fast forward to the backside of Calvary. Jesus has now hung, bled and died on the cross. He has been placed in a borrowed tomb and, just as He said, He rose early on the first day of the week. He is now about to ascend to heaven and return to the Father, but before He leaves the earthly realm on a cloud, He gives the disciples an assignment! Matthew records that He says, "Go . . . and make disciples" (Matthew 28:19). Note that He is speaking to His *disciples* when He says, "Go make *disciples*." A. W. Tozer seems to have received this revelation. Tozer said, "Only a disciple can make a disciple." The assignment given to the disciples is to go make disciples.

I am both amazed and grieved that it appears that much of the Church today has lost sight of the target of discipleship as the assignment—the "commission"—given to us by Christ. I asked a dear friend, who leads an international network of over 1,500 churches—to give me the names of two or three ministries that are doing well in making disciples. He sent me back the names of three churches that he said are doing a "pretty fair" job. I wrote back and said, "I don't want someone who is doing a 'fair' job. I want someone who has it down and is doing a good job. I don't want to reinvent the wheel. I want to learn from someone who is doing it." He wrote back a two-word email: "Good luck." He said he doesn't really know anyone who is doing a "good job." His response indicated what I had also observed: Discipleship is not a clearly stated goal in the Church of today.

I took a class at the University of Illinois that I repeatedly cut. I cut that class every way but loose! About three weeks before the end of the semester, almost by accident, I discovered as I perused the syllabus that the final paper was due in about a week. It was one of those classes where your entire grade was based on one paper. I made my way to the library. Burned the midnight oil. Crammed for about three days. After pulling an all-nighter typing on my typewriter (we didn't have computers in those days!), I proudly turned in the paper on time. A few days later, the professor returned the papers. I knew I was in trouble when I saw that he had written notes on the cover page! His words were positive: "Good paper. Good content. Good research." But the grade was *F*—and the *F* was in red ink! I really thought it was a bit of overkill to put the *F* in red; an *F* is just as much an *F* in black ink! Then I noticed that there was an additional note at the bottom of the cover page. The professor had written, "This was NOT the assignment!" Wow! Good paper. Good content. Good research. Grade *F*—because this was NOT the assignment.

We live in an age of "megas": mega-ministries, mega-churches and mega-buildings. However, I fear that many of us will stand before our Lord and say, "We welcomed many members. We built many buildings. We offered great music. We trained great praise leaders." We have done all these impressive things, but I wonder how many of us have broken the chain of spiritual succession. Disciples make disciples. Maybe we have made more members than disciples. Certainly disciples are members of the Body of Christ. Certainly disciples praise and worship. But maybe it is time to intentionally, strategically and consciously return to the assignment given to us by the risen Christ. Maybe we should place disciple-making at the top of our mission statements. Jesus gave a trans-generational assignment. He commissioned and challenged His disciples to make disciples. Tozer would agree.

57

FROM POSSESSOR
TO POSSESSION

BRUCE WILKINSON
Bestselling Author, *The Prayer of Jabez*

There is within the human heart a tough, fibrous root of fallen
life whose nature is to possess, always to possess.
A. W. TOZER

A beautiful and holy upheaval happens in the life of a Christian.
For us, victory begins with God-in-flesh hanging from a splintered
beam. We find our life only by losing it for His sake (see Matthew
16:25). We are told that the "poor in spirit" are the ones who possess the kingdom of heaven (see Matthew 5:3). This ancient and
living faith is rich with paradox; a glorious reordering of our inner
world begins with a fall, a cross, loss, death and the burial of an old
nature. Then comes grace in all its scandal and brightness, bringing redemption, freedom and life. Death has lost its sting (see 1 Corinthians 15:55). A new nature begins.

At the Cross, this "fibrous root of fallen life whose nature is to
possess" is juxtaposed with a God who freely gives all things. Christ,
the second Adam, heals the rift caused by the possessive nature of
the first Adam. Suddenly, we are beggars invited to a feast. We are
sinners who become sons, co-heirs and rulers of a new Kingdom.
Christ invites us to join Him: "If any man will come after me, let

him deny himself, and take up his cross, and follow me" (Matthew 16:24, *KJV*). The cross, this time carried on *our* backs, still paves the way to freedom. Through loss we find unfathomable joy!

"The kingdom of heaven is like treasure hidden in a field. When a man found it, he hid it again, and then *in his joy* went and sold *all he had* and bought that field" (Matthew 13:44, *NIV*, emphasis added). The man who sold all he had did so *in joy* because, compared to the treasure in the field, what he forfeited could not be termed "loss" at all. This former root of possessiveness—this deep disease of hoarding, calculating and selfishness—is exposed as hollow pursuit when it meets the extravagant nature of grace. Life in Christ does not clamor and scramble to gain possessions for itself—or even for possession of self. We shed the old skin and become lost in Him. We no longer are the possessors; we have become His possession. We have a new identity. This is no surface change—no delicate and polite transformation. It is magnificent! We are redeemed from slavery to freedom—from possessors to possession.

Many grow uncomfortable with the terminology of "loss," "denial" or "poor" and wonder how this could possibly be the path to abundant life. But could anything about our old life, now buried with Christ, be considered *loss*? Slavery to sin? Penalty of death? Separation from God? A kingdom of darkness? We lose this old reality and in its place are given freedom, life and intimacy with the living God in a Kingdom of glorious light. What a beautiful trade this is! As we follow our King into this cross-life of forsaking our former frenzy of possessing, may we find the freedom and joy of losing all to gain the kingdom of heaven—the treasure in a field. As Tozer reminds us, "Though free from all sense of possessing, [we] yet possess *all* things."

"Blessed be the God and Father of our Lord Jesus Christ, who has blessed us in Christ *with every spiritual blessing in the heavenly places*" (Ephesians 1:3, *ESV*, emphasis added)!

58

THE DANGERS OF CHASING THE WIND

STEPHEN CHRISTIAN
Lead Vocalist, Anberlin

If the Holy Spirit was withdrawn from the church today,
95 percent of what we do would go on and no one would know
the difference. If the Holy Spirit had been withdrawn from the
New Testament church, 95 percent of what they did would stop,
and everybody would know the difference.

A. W. TOZER

I remember it quite well: I was in the hallway to exit a venue in Spokane, Washington, when a tall young woman wearing glasses walked up to me, bearing a gift in her right hand. It was a small blue paperback with clouds covering half the cover. The book was well-worn; it had obviously been read and loved. She explained that no other book had taught her so much or opened her mind to the idea of God as greatly as this handbook had done.

I must admit that when I hear that something or someone has completely changed a person's life or outlook, I am a bit skeptical. Thus, the book remained in my suitcase for quite some time. However, on a long plane ride (more or less by default), I began to read it. Almost immediately, my skepticism waned, and I became a believer in this author's works as well. That book led me to a deeper longing to understand the unending depth of God—and I also felt compelled to research this new character who was pushing me forward in my discipleship: A. W. Tozer.

One of the passages I later read that stood out and stayed with me was the pointed commentary from A. W. Tozer given above on the modern-day Church. It is perhaps more true now than ever. Our projects and building funds are moving ahead swimmingly. We know the hymns by heart. We know when the offering is going to be taken. Even the pastor knows how long he has to preach before the congregation gets hungry and begins giving him notice by frequently staring at their timepieces. It seems that we are nearing autopilot with our church life and fellowship experience.

I grew up attending a church in Winter Haven, Florida, and this quote adequately summed up most of my experience there. They were so hungry for the latest trend in Christian circles that they passed over the real object of their search. I remember piling into vans and driving six or more hours north to experience what this or that church was implementing. More than once, our pastor, staff members and others from the congregation flew internationally to learn and adopt their counterparts' ways; on returning, they attempted to reenact the same "revival" they had witnessed abroad on our humble local congregation.

> Then a great and powerful wind tore the mountains apart and shattered the rocks before the LORD, but the LORD was not in the wind. After the wind there was an earthquake, but the LORD was not in the earthquake. After the earthquake came a fire, but the LORD was not in the fire. And after the fire came a gentle whisper (1 Kings 19:11-12, *NIV*).

Our diminutive church read all the latest literature and seemed to jump on every book bandwagon reported by Christian magazines to be making a big splash in other churches around the world. Yet nothing ever seemed to catch, and within a few years of my departure from the church, it crumbled. I am not saying that these people were not good people, or that they were without good intent. What I am saying is that many of them were looking everywhere but to the Holy Spirit for their guidance and knowledge of the holy.

They had their systems in place, the proper praise and worship songs were sung, and the leadership even met with and sat under the teaching of pastors whose congregations were experiencing God's presence in powerful ways. What they missed out on is exactly what the Early Church knew and adhered to: openness to the moving of the Holy Spirit. He is not always in the mighty earthquakes and winds; in fact, He can usually be found in the gentle whisper.

If the Holy Spirit withdrew from the Church, I wonder how many years it would take before we noticed? Books would still be written and published in the name of God, and songs would still be composed and sung in His honor, but deep inside our well-organized programs and vision statements there would be us—beautiful, elegant, well-read and well-composed whitewashed tombs.

How I long to return to the days when God's people relied not on a formula heard in a podcast but rather on the urging of the God who dwells within us. I desire that each of us would follow not a man or woman who claims to know how to find spirituality but the Christ who died and rose again so that we might know grace and salvation. May we not pursue the works of the Holy Spirit in other countries, in trends, in fads, or in the latest and greatest praise and worship record, but instead immerse ourselves in the presence of the Holy Spirit who dwells with (and within) us here at home.

Seek ye first the kingdom of God . . .
and all these things shall be added unto you.
MATTHEW 6:33, *KJV*

59

RISKY BUSINESS

KRIS VALLOTTON
Author and Senior Associate Pastor, Bethel Church,
Redding, California

Our walk by faith, if it is true biblical faith, will get us into trouble.
A. W. TOZER

Real faith is spelled R-I-S-K. The very nature of a true Christian is that we are led not by logic and reason, but by the Spirit. Our hearts will take us places our heads would never go. Yet allowing the Spirit to guide us through life is dangerous business. Thousands of years ago, Solomon, the wisest king to ever grace this planet, put it like this: "Where no oxen are, the manger is clean, but much revenue comes by the strength of the ox" (Proverbs 14:4, *NASB*). It's impossible to walk with God and not make messes, because courageous disciples don't give *preeminence* to "common sense."

This way of approaching life in the Kingdom is not new. It's actually demonstrated throughout the entire Bible. From Gideon's army of 300 pitcher-carrying soldiers, to Elisha's floating axe head, or Joshua's seven-day march around an enemy city, the Word of God is filled with irrational stories that defy common reason. We often share these stories as awesome historic tales of the God who does the unreasonable, the irrational and the impossible. But it never occurs to some of us that God still requires His people to live lives that transcend our understanding and invites us into His miraculous interventions.

Resistance to experiencing the impossible interventions of God has resulted in many believers being educated out of obedience. They exchange God's works for good deeds, reducing "Jesus people" to nice, friendly citizens instead of fire-breathing world changers. They have domesticated the Lion of the tribe of Judah. Many of our churches have become zoos—artificial places where people go to be entertained by the lions. It's hard to be ready for the jungle when you train in the zoo!

It takes incredible courage to be a follower of Jesus and not just a believer in Christ. In fact, the book of Revelation says that the *cowards* aren't going to heaven (see Revelation 21:8). So, until we have something to die for, we really never live. Jesus put it best: "For whoever wishes to save his life will lose it; but whoever loses his life for My sake will find it" (Matthew 16:25, *NASB*). We are all terminal! We are all going to die someday; we just don't know when. The real question is: Will we really ever live? I am not talking about taking up space and sucking in air; I mean really living—making a difference, pushing past our fear and taking hold of our destiny. Until we deal with death, we don't really ever live. The writer of Hebrews said, "Therefore, since the children share in flesh and blood, He Himself likewise also partook of the same, that through death He might render powerless him who had the power of death, that is, the devil, and might free those who through fear of death were subject to slavery all their lives" (Hebrews 2:14-15, *NASB*).

It is only when we accept the inevitable that we can actually do the impossible. When a person loses the fear of death, he or she begins to move into new realms of impact. An ancient Roman adage puts it like this: "A coward dies a thousand deaths, but a brave man dies only once!" The life we were called to live lies on the other side of our fears. Remember, God didn't childproof the Garden. He isn't as interested in keeping us safe as He is in trying to keep us from a meaningless life. Courage is a catalyst to a life full of purpose.

Queen Esther is a great example of someone who had to step over the "chicken line" to do God's will—which in Esther's case was to save her people. When Mordecai first tried to enlist Esther in the struggle to save the Jews, she was terrified and tried to resist her calling. Then Mordecai sent this famous message to Esther: "Do not imagine that you in the king's palace can escape any more than all the Jews. For if you remain silent at this time, relief and deliverance will arise for the Jews from another place and you and your father's house will perish. And who knows whether you have not attained royalty for such a time as this?" (Esther 4:13-14, NASB). Finally Esther got a grip on her fear and replied, "Go, assemble all the Jews who are found in Susa, and fast for me; do not eat or drink for three days, night or day. I and my maidens also will fast in the same way. And thus I will go in to the king, which is not according to the law; and if I perish, I perish" (Esther 4:16, NASB).

Queen Esther was stressed out, but she refused to let her fear dictate her future. She entered the palace and appealed to her king. She won the king's favor, and he hung Haman on the gallows that Haman had erected for Mordecai. Esther rescued the Jews and saved the day.

The dogs of doom often stand at the doors of our destiny. They start barking when we are about to step over the "chicken line" and cross the threshold into our God-given purpose. Most people never fully enter into their promised land because they allow fear to dictate the boundaries of their future. They reduce their lives to accommodate the dogs and mistake the silence for peace. For example, maybe you are afraid to fly, so you never get on a plane. You won't feel scared, because you have scaled back your life to silence the dogs. You may think you are absolutely tranquil, but the truth is that you are still full of fear. Subconsciously, you know that flying will awaken the sleeping monster, and he will torment you until you slay him or obey him.

It's time we become troublemakers! We are called to destroy the works of the devil. When we live only by logic and reason, we render ourselves predictable and thereby easily undermined and defeated. But when we are led by the Spirit and put on the full armor of God, we operate in stealth—hidden in Christ—and our archenemy has no idea how to resist us, because he doesn't possess the mind of Christ. Take a risk and start dying to live. A hundred years from now, you'll be glad you did.

THE PERFECT
LOVE STORY

LAUREN BARLOW
Drummer and Singer, BarlowGirl

*God is so vastly wonderful, so utterly and completely delightful that He
can, without anything other than Himself, meet and overflow the deepest
demands of our total nature, mysterious and deep as that nature is.*
A. W. TOZER

Love.

Love is a very powerful thing.

There are a million and one emotions and feelings wrapped
around that one little word. It can make you the happiest you've
ever been in your entire life, but it also has the power to break your
heart.

It's exciting and scary all at the same time.

It's that feeling that your heart is about to beat out of your
chest.

It's tears and it's laughter.

It's that feeling that someone knows you to the core of your
being and accepts you just the way you are.

That's true love.

There really is no better feeling in this world.

To love and to be loved right back.

The feeling of being completed. That there is that someone in your life who is everything you need and more. To have someone be there for you at any moment of the day or night. Someone who will listen to you no matter what you have to say—not because they have to, but because they want to.

A good part of each of our lives is spent in search of that one person who will make us feel all those things.

The songs we sing are written about it.

The movies we watch make us want our own love stories to look just like what we see on the screen.

We long to have the perfect love story.

Till death do us part.

But I must ask us all a question: Can one single person in this world fulfill every need, want and feeling that we've ever had inside ourselves?

Now maybe that question is simply rhetorical, because we all know we are imperfect people. As convincing as I may have sounded with my "love speech," you need to know something about me. This may come as a shock to you, but I have never been in love with anyone. Other than a crazy 14-year-old boy proposing to me at a concert, I've never had someone tell me that they are in love with me, and I have yet to tell someone that myself.

Okay, I'll just go ahead and say it: I've never even had a boyfriend. Yes, I actually made that choice in my life; it wasn't something that was forced upon me. I'm not complaining (or using this book to find a husband). The decision to give up recreational dating was all my own, and I don't regret it. Allow me to explain.

You know that feeling of wanting something so badly you will do whatever it takes to get it?

You wanna play the game, you gotta practice.

You wanna be fit, you better work your tail off at the gym.

If I want to be the drummer in my band, I have to put in the time to learn the drums and be good—or I'm gonna be replaced.

We know that in order for us to attain the things we desperately want in this life, we have to be willing to sacrifice something else.

When I was a child, my parents instilled in me a strong desire for God and the things of God. I was taught that I should never let anything get in the way of discovering exactly what God wanted for me in my life. I had—and still have—a deep hunger to know God, and I decided early on that I was never going to let anything get in the way of knowing Him. So yes, the dating age in my house was 16 years old, but as that time grew closer, my sisters and I decided to ask God if that was something we should do.

That's right, we actually asked God if we should date.

Silly, I know—but after much prayer and research, we came to the realization that recreational dating was only going to get in the way of our story with God. We understood that our young years were instrumental to finding out who we were in God, and that dating around was simply going to distract from that goal. I was 16. I wasn't ready to be married; I was just going to date to have fun. Because my desire to know God was stronger than that, I put dating on the back burner. I have spent my life finding my definition in God—not in a guy. To me, dating would simply have been a distraction from following after God with my whole heart.

My story with Him has been one of the most incredible journeys of my life.

I always think it's kind of strange that we go to everyone else to find out who we are, when He is the One who created us in the first place. Shouldn't we be going to Him first? In the moments when I feel horrible about myself—or maybe I've done something wrong—He is the One to whom I have learned to run.

And He listens.

Every time.

Then there are those incredible times when He speaks to me in my pain or when I need a word from Him. He truly is always there for me. He knows me fully and completely and loves me just the same.

There is no better feeling in the world.

Now, I'm not trying to judge anyone. I know that roughly 95 percent of the people in this world do date—and the other 5 percent will once they get a little older. This is simply my story. This is the way I chose to discover and know God's love in my life.

We all have different stories.

But I wouldn't trade my story with Him for the world.

That is not to say that this has been an easy journey. I don't want you to think my path has been all sunshine and rainbows. It's been hard. Sacrifice is never easy. The beautiful thing is that the end result always outweighs the sacrifice.

There have been moments when I have felt completely broken and woefully incomplete. Times when I thought no one, not even God, could love a person like me. But because my life has been a journey of discovering His love, I always run back to Him (although sometimes it takes awhile) and ask Him what He thinks about me.

I've learned how to hear His voice and even to find comfort in the silences. I've learned that whatever I need, He is the answer. There is no one else I need to run to. This isn't meant to sound cliché or religious. He simply is my passion.

This path with Him has been one like no other, and the wonderful thing is that it has only just begun.

Tozer-Grams

In the early 1940s, Tozer was a rising figure in the evangelical movement of his day—not yet well known, but definitely on his way. During this time, Tozer started writing occasional articles for *The Alliance Weekly*, the official magazine of the Christian and Missionary Alliance. His writings were well received, and the editor invited Tozer to contribute on a more regular basis. For about five years, Tozer wrote a weekly column called "Tozer-Grams," which were pithy, sometimes humorous, and always widely quoted within the denomination. Here are some never-before-published "Tozer-Grams." As always with Tozer, they leave you feeling challenged and convicted to know God more. Hope you enjoy!

Heaven Is Not a Garbage Pail

There's a cheap, modern idea that we go to heaven by a kind of "drop a nickel in the slot, pull down the lever and take out your ticket" mechanism—that if I accept Jesus, I go to heaven, and if I don't accept Him, I go to hell. I heard a man on the radio the other day, not long ago, trying to make it very plain that it doesn't require righteousness to go to heaven—it requires nothing but accepting Jesus. Well, what this man forgot was that the act of accepting Christ, if it is indeed a true act of accepting Christ, has an instant effect upon the whole moral life. It changes a man from being a bad man to being a good man.

It is ridiculous to say that heaven is the garbage pail for all the wickedness of men—that by grace the Lord takes foulness in. No king ever took the garbage pail into the king's parlor. Likewise, God is not going by some trick of grace to take evil, foul-minded, self-righteous and vile people into His heaven. When He saves a man, He saves him from sin—and if he's not saved from sin, he's not saved at all. There is no act of grace and no trick of mercy or of justification that can take an unholy man into the presence of God, or take an evil man into God's holy heaven.

Jesus "did not come to call the righteous, but sinners" (Matthew 9:13). That is, He came not to call people who thought they were righteous, but people who knew they were sinful. However, when He calls us to Himself and saves us, He saves us out of our past and out of our iniquity—and by the threefold act of justification, regeneration and sanctification, He makes people fit for heaven. It is absurd, this idea that justification is imparted righteousness—that it is a robe of righteousness put over a dirty, filthy fellow who terribly needs a bath, and that that dirty filthy fellow, filled with cooties and the accumulations of dirt of his lifetime, will stand boldly in God Almighty's holy heaven among seraphim, cherubim, archangels and the spirits of just men made perfect, and glibly and flippantly say, "I belong in hell. I'm a filthy man. What are you going to do about it? I have on me the robe of Christ's righteousness and that's enough." This is a heresy as terrible and devastating as the heresy promulgated by the falsely called Jehovah's Witnesses.

God saves only sinners, and saves only sinners who know they're sinners, and saves only sinners who admit they're sinners, but He saves sinners from being sinners, to being good men and full of the Holy Ghost. When we teach anything else, we're teaching heresy—a frightful heresy.

CHOICES AND CONSEQUENCES

Everything we are is a result of choices we've made. Everything we are today is a result of choices we made yesterday, and everything we will be tomorrow will be the result of choices we make today. Those choices may be good, or they may be bad. They may be ignorant, or they may be well-advised. They may be impulsive, or they may be made after much thought. They may be made out of spite. Many a pair of lovers has had a blow-up and a fight, and the girl rushed out and married somebody else and said, "I'll show that twerp." Then she lived with her second choice for a lifetime and whispered to people who knew her in years to come, "This was the mistake of my life." Selfish choices and cowardly choices; choices that are made because we're afraid to make other ones and careful choices;

wise, unselfish, far-seen courageous choices; humble, faith-inspired, God-obeying choices—we can make all of those. When we make a choice today, we are deciding who we will be tomorrow.

Resisting the World's Propaganda

The greatest war today is the war to win control of our minds. The greatest war that ever was fought is not in history books anywhere. It was not fought during the Second World War, nor in Korea, nor in the First World War, nor in the Revolutionary, the Civil, or any of the wars that have bloodied the pages of history. Those wars were wars of body against body, gun against gun, sword against sword, battalion against battalion.

No, the greatest war in the world is the battle for our minds—and that is being waged today by every modern, effective technique. It is being waged by the press. If you could suddenly stand off objectively and look at your own mind and see how much the press has fed into your mind and how you have come to be more or less a creature of the press, you'd be shocked, I'm sure, and you'd spend days in fasting and prayer to get free from it. Another technique being used is that of the school system. Without a school system, of course, we would be barbarians and heathens. It must exist. We must have our schools. Then there's the radio, which is a new technique for the dissemination of ideas. It is also being used to help control our minds. Of course there is the drama, which has always been, in its various forms, an effective technique for the controlling of the minds of the people.

Then we have developed, over the last 50 or 60 years, in America, one of the most potent techniques ever devised by the mind of man for the control of the mass thinking of the people—and that is advertising. The advertisers are the best educators in the world, and they're busy educating us by every means they know—expensive and carefully thought-out means. They are busy controlling our thinking. Now the object, of course, is to win everyone to think the same way on certain subjects—certain great topics in life, such as love and money and pleasure and marriage and values and religion and the future and God and our relation to God and all the rest. People are being influenced very strongly by these means to think the same about virtually every aspect of life.

WHO CONTROLS OUR PHILOSOPHY?

Everybody's a philosopher. Only some get the reputation for being philosophers, but everybody's a philosopher—everybody. The gangster's a philosopher, and the kid who carries a switch-blade and attacks an innocent kid on the street and kills him or cuts him up—he's a philosopher too. If you press him and push him into a corner, he'll come through with reasons to explain why he did what he did—and reasons are philosophy. Wherever you have reason for doing, and do, you are a philosopher. So everybody's a philosopher, and we have certain philosophies of life, or a certain philosophy of life. We look out upon life and see it from a certain viewpoint—that is philosophy, and that makes us philosophers. Whether we write great big books and call ourselves by that name or are simple people who would smile at the thought that we're philosophers, we're all philosophers, nevertheless.

Now, who's going to control our philosophy? Who's going to determine our outlook upon life? Who's going to decide? You say, "I do that myself." Oh, don't make me laugh, brother. You don't do that yourself at all, you only think you do. I would only think I did, if I indeed didn't know that I didn't. Then we have to have our viewpoint on love. What is this love business anyhow? All you have to do is press a button, and someone will be telling you what it is and what it isn't. That's how we get our ideas about human love—love between the sexes and love in our society. We get that from the radio. We get it from the newspaper and from the press generally and from advertising. Then, when it comes to such things as money, we think of money what the press tells us to think of money, what the radio suggests we think of money, or what we have learned at school about money. Similarly, when it comes to pleasures . . . our attitude towards life, towards pleasures, towards just about anything—innocent or harmful, either one or both—we learn from the world. Worldly influences control our minds. They get us to thinking about things the way they want us to think, and they do it, I say, by means of the press, school, radio, drama, advertising and perhaps a few other minor techniques. Our views about religion and values and the future and God—those, of course, are the most important. What I think about money is important, but what I think about God is still more important, and there has not been a time, probably, since the Great Awakening under Jonathan Edwards, when there was more religion in the country than there is now. Yes, there is much religion, and religious thought, but we must ask ourselves who is directing our thinking about religion—God or the media?

WHO IS THE HOLY SPIRIT?

The fellowship of the Church has degenerated into a social fellowship with a mild religious flavor. For me, either I want God or I do not want anything at all to do with religion. I could never get interested in some old maids' social club with a little bit of Christianity thrown in to give it respectability. Either I want it all or I do not want any. I want God or I am perfectly happy to go out and be something else. I think the Lord had something like that in mind when He said, "I know thy works, that thou art neither cold nor hot: I would thou wert cold or hot" (Revelation 3:15, *KJV*).

A terrible result of the failure to honor the Holy Ghost is that so many non-spiritual, un-spiritual and anti-spiritual features have been brought into the Church. The average church today could not run on a hymnbook and a Bible. The Church started out with a Bible and then developed a hymnbook—and for years, that was enough. Now, some people could not serve God without at least one vanload of equipment to keep them happy. All this attraction to win people and keep them coming may be fine—it may be elevated, it may be cheap, it may be degrading, it may be coarse, it may be artistic, but it all depends on who is running the show. Because the Holy Spirit is not the center of attraction, and the

Lord is not the one in charge, we must bring in all sorts of anti-scriptural and un-scriptural claptrap to make the people happy and keep them coming back.

The horrible part is not so much that this is true, but that it needs to be at all. The great woe is not the presence of religious toys and trifles, but the necessity for them because the presence of the eternal Spirit is not in our midst. The tragedy and woe of the hour is trying to make up for His absence by doing these things to keep our own spirits up.

If the Church said it and the Scripture did not say it, I would reject it. I would not believe an archangel if he came to me with a wingspread of 12 feet and shining like an atom bomb just at the moment it goes off, if he could not give me chapter and verse. I want to know it is here in the Book.

I am not a traditionalist. If anybody comes to me and says, "This is traditional," I will say, "All right, that is interesting if true, but is it true? Give me chapter and verse." All tradition must bow in reverence before the clear testimony of God's Word.

What I want to know is this: Were these old brethren when they said all this, telling the truth? Well, listen to what the Scriptures have to say.

The Scripture says the Holy Spirit is God, giving to Him the attributes that belong to God the Son and God the Father. For instance, Psalm 139 says, "Whither shall I go from thy spirit? or whither shall I flee from thy presence?" (v. 7, *KJV*). That is omnipresence. Not even the devil is omnipresent. Only God can claim omnipresence. The psalmist attributed omnipresence to the Holy Spirit.

What is the Spirit? Who is the Spirit? How do we know who the Spirit is? We know by the Scriptures; we know because the Church Fathers knew what the Scriptures said. Unless He is feelingly in our midst, unless He is consciously in our midst, He might as well be somewhere else. It is possible to run a church without the Holy Spirit, which is the terrible thing. You organize it. You get a board, a pastor, a choir, a ladies' aid society and a Sunday School, and you get all organized. I believe in organization. I am not against it, I am for it. But sometimes we get organized, and we get a pastor to turn the crank, and that is all there is to it. The Holy Ghost can leave, and the pastor goes on turning the crank, and nobody finds it out for five years. Oh, what a horrible tragedy to the Church of Christ!

But, we do not have to have it that way. This kind of preaching is going to do one of two things. There is going to be a reaction against it, or there is going to be an eager seeking. I'm praying and believing the latter will be the case. I believe that there will be an eager seeking for better things than what we now have.

God's Word to the Church today is that the restoration of the Spirit to His rightful place in the life of the Church is by all means the most important thing that could possibly take place.

PROMISE OF THE FATHER

It is quite difficult to get a Christian over the fear of the Holy Spirit. By that, I do not mean reverence for Him. You cannot reverence the Holy Spirit too much, but you can be overly afraid of Him. I am sure many people are afraid of the Holy Spirit. But if you remember, He is the Father's promise, given to us as a gift. Imagine a man promises his son a bicycle for Christmas, and the boy remembers and comes back and reminds the father. Nobody is ever afraid of a promise of a father who loves him.

The members of the redeemed Church should be bound in the bundle of love for the Holy Spirit. The truth is, God never thought of His Church apart from the Holy Spirit. We are born of the Spirit, we are baptized into the Body of Christ by the Spirit, we are anointed with the Spirit, we are led of the Spirit, we are taught by the Spirit, and the Spirit is the medium—the divine solution—in which God holds His Church. The hymnist portrayed the Holy Spirit as the "essence of the godhead uncreated." God never dreamed of His people apart from the Holy Spirit and accordingly made promises to them.

The period of the realization came suddenly: The Father fulfilled His promise, and the expectations were fully met and more.

Always remember this: God is always bigger than anything God can say, because words are inadequate to express God and what God can do. Any promise God ever makes, God has to fulfill it. The reason being that God is so great—His heart so kind and His desire so intense and tremendous—that language does not express it. Not the Greek, not the English—no language expresses God. It cannot. If language could contain God, then language would be equal to God.

So everything God says in the Bible must be understood to be a little greater than what we read, even as God is greater than language. God promised the disciples that they should receive power, and that power should be an afflatus from heaven above which should come upon them, cross the threshold of their spirits, enter the depths of their souls and dwell there forever. This power should work within them, lead them, purify them, instruct them and teach them. We have to believe that the fulfillment will be greater than the promise, because the fulfillment is of God and the promise is mere words.

They also insist that at conversion we receive what the disciples received back there at Pentecost. I want to ask you, have you ever seen anybody who received at his conversion what Peter received in the upper chamber? Have you ever met anybody like that? Do you know anybody like that? When you were converted, did you have the power Peter had when he preached? Didn't the average Christian in the Early Church have something that apparently we do not have in this day? I think they did.

Is modern fundamentalism a satisfactory fulfillment of the expectation raised by the Father and Christ? Our heavenly Father promised the gift of the Holy Ghost to come upon His children. Jesus promised that we should have the Spirit—that He would come, and that He should take the things of Christ and make them known unto us. He should bring all things to our memory. We should have power when the Spirit came. He promised all this, and I look around at cold, dead, dried-up fundamentalism. It is textualism hanging out to dry. Then they want me to believe that what we have is what they had back then. I just cannot do it. We Christians now are a scrub lot compared to those Christians back there.

Does your heart, personally, witness that what you now enjoy is what our Lord promised to His people? Does your heart bear witness that what you now have is all that God meant when He painted that wonderful picture of the fullness of the Spirit? Or is there something more for the Church?

Set aside time and search the Scriptures. If the Scriptures do not convince you that the Church and the individuals in the Church ought to be living a happy, Spirit-filled life, then do not listen to me. Because if I preach for five hours straight, but I do not preach according to the truth found in the Bible, then I am wrong no matter how eloquent I try to be. But if what I have been saying is supported by what you find in the Scriptures, then we should be crying out to God for a fuller experience of His Holy Spirit in our lives. Pray, yield, believe, obey and see what God will do for you over the next weeks.

Contributors

Adam Agee

Adam Agee is the lead singer and guitarist for the Christian pop band Stellar Kart. Before forming the band in 2001, he was a youth worship leader from Phoenix, Arizona, teaming up with fellow Stellar Kart member Jordan Messer. In 2007, Stellar Kart's single "Me and Jesus" received the Dove Award as Christian rock/contemporary song of the year.

stellarkart.com
twitter.com/stellarkartband
facebook.com/stellarkart

Jane Albright

Jane Albright is the head women's basketball coach at the University of Nevada. She has coached four different teams to a combined nine NCAA Tournaments and four WNIT bids, including the 2000 championship at Wisconsin. Albright is a four-time conference coach of the year and a two-time district IV coach of the year. She is still the all-time wins leader at both Wisconsin and Northern Illinois. Jane contributed an essay in *The Greatest Leader Ever* by the Fellowship of Christian Athletes.

nevadawolfpack.com

Nancy Alcorn

Nancy Alcorn spent the first eight years of her career working for the state of Tennessee. It was during this time of government work that Nancy realized the inadequacy of social programs to offer real transformation in the lives of troubled individuals. Nancy realized that only Christ could truly change a life, so she started Mercy Ministries in 1983. Since that time, under Nancy's leadership, numerous residential and outreach programs have been established in various locations across America and other nations around the world, and the ministry continues to grow and expand. Nancy is an author, and she frequently speaks at conferences around the world. She resides in Nashville, Tennessee, which is also the home of the national headquarters of Mercy Ministries.

mercyministries.org
twitter.com/nancyalcorn

RANDY ALCORN

Randy Alcorn is the founder of Eternal Perspective Ministries and the bestselling author of more than 40 books, with four million in print. His nonfiction books include *Heaven* and *If God Is Good,* and his fiction books include *Deadline, Dominion* and *Deception.* His greatest joy is spending time with his wife and best friend, Nanci, and their family (including his four precious grandsons). He also enjoys reading, research, biking and tennis.

epm.org
randyalcorn.blogspot.com/
twitter.com/randyalcorn

ALYSSA BARLOW

Alyssa Barlow (of BarlowGirl) is in love with Jesus, and that's her greatest accomplishment.

barlowgirl.com
twitter.com/alyssabarlow

REBECCA BARLOW

Rebecca Barlow has been traveling the world with her two sisters for

the last 12 years in BarlowGirl. She has a desire to see the brokenhearted healed and has committed her life to God for that purpose.

barlowgirl.com
twitter.com/rebeccabarlow

VINCE AND MARYANN BARLOW

Vincent and MaryAnn Barlow have four children, are the parents and managers of BarlowGirl, and grandparents to their son and daughter-in-law's five incredible children. They are both former staff members of Willow Creek Community Church. When not on the road with their daughters, they reside in the Chicago area.

WES AND DAVID BEAVIS

 Wes Beavis is an Australian-born motivational speaker and author. He is a graduate of Sydney College of Divinity and has spent the last 25 years traveling the world, inspiring people to make the most of their God-given lives and opportunities. Wes lives in Irvine, California, with his wife, Ellie, and their two sons, David and Zack.

wesbeavis.com

 David Beavis is a student at Vanguard University of Southern California. He also serves as a student campus pastor. In his spare time, David enjoys spending time with friends, reading and playing basketball.

LISA BEVERE

 Lisa Bevere is an international speaker, bestselling author and co-host of "The Messenger" television program, which broadcasts in more than 200 countries. Since 1996, Lisa has written many bestselling books, including *Fight Like a Girl, Kissed the Girls and Made Them Cry, Nurture*, and *Out of Control and Loving It*. Lisa and her husband, John, also a bestselling author and speaker, founded Messenger International (www.MessengerInter national.org), an organization in Orlando, Florida, founded to inspire godliness and release people into fulfilled lives in Christ. Lisa and John reside in Colorado Springs, Colorado, and enjoy

spending time with their four sons, stunning daughter-in-law, and adorable grandbaby.

twitter.com/lisabevere
facebook.com/lisabevere.page
messengerinternational.blogspot.com/
messengerint.org

MIKE BICKLE

Mike Bickle is the director of the International House of Prayer Missions Base of Kansas City (IHOP-KC). IHOP-KC is an evangelical missions organization based on 24/7 prayer, with worship that is engaged in many evangelistic and inner city outreaches, multiple justice initiatives, planting houses of prayer, and training missionaries. Mike is the author of several books including *Passion for Jesus, Growing in the Prophetic, The Pleasures of Loving God, After God's Own Heart,* and *Prayers to Strengthen Your Inner Man.*

mikebickle.org   ihop.org
twitter.com/mikebickle

DAVID CARR

David Carr is the drummer for the Grammy-Award-winning Christian band Third Day. David started playing for Third Day when he was still in high school. He was born in Atlanta, Georgia.

twitter.com/davidcarr3d
thirdday.com

MICHAEL CATT

Michael Catt has been the senior pastor of Sherwood Baptist Church in Albany, Georgia, since 1989. He is the author of several books, including *Courageous Living* and the ReFRESH® book series with Broadman & Holman. Michael is the editor of www.2ProphetU.com, a resource website for pastors developed with Warren Wiersbe, and the founder of ReFRESH® (www.ReFRESHconference.org), a conference on revival and spiritual awakening. Michael also serves as executive producer for the films developed by Sherwood Pictures. Michael and his wife, Terri, have two grown daughters, Erin and Hayley.

> michaelcatt.com
> sherwoodbaptist.net
> twitter.com/michaelcatt

STEPHEN CHRISTIAN

 Stephen Christian is the lead vocalist of the alternative rock band Anberlin. He is also one of the main songwriters of the band, along with Joseph Milligan. Christian co-founded Faceless International along with his two friends, Seth Cain and Sarah Freeman. Faceless is a non-profit organization focused on fighting human trafficking and modern-day slavery. Christian currently resides in Nashville, Tennessee.

> anberlin.com
> facelessinternational.com
> twitter.com/stephenanberlin

SHANE CLAIBORNE

 Shane Claiborne is an author and activist, and one of the founders of The Simple Way. The Simple Way is an intentional community in north Philadelphia that has helped birth and connect radical faith communities and movements for peace across the globe. Shane authored *The Irresistible Revolution* and co-authored *Jesus for President* (with Chris Haw), *Follow Me to Freedom* (with John M. Perkins) and *Common Prayer* (with Jonathan Wilson-Hartgrove and Enuma Okoro).

> thesimpleway.org
> facebook.com/shaneclaiborne

PAUL CLARK

Paul Clark is recognized as one of the founding fathers of the Jesus Movement and the Contemporary Christian Music industry. During his 13-year association with Word Records in the 1970s and 1980s, Paul's songwriting, record producing and avant-garde artistry placed him in the forefront along with artists like Phil Keaggy, Second Chapter of Acts, Love Song, Larry Norman, Andre Crouch, Honeytree, Keith Green, Randy Stonehill, Barry McGuire and many others. Paul has completed 17 solo recording projects, including *Approaching Jerusalem, Hand to the Plow* and *Songs from the Savior*. He has written more than 400 songs, produced records for several artists, served as a worship leader/pastor, and has been an author and published photographer. Today, Paul continues to tour, perform, lead worship, fervently serve Jesus and encourage people around the world.

paulclarkmusic.com

JONI EARECKSON TADA

 Joni Eareckson Tada, founder and CEO of Joni and Friends International Disability Center, is an international advocate for people with disabilities. A diving accident in 1967 left Joni Eareckson, then 17, a quadriplegic in a wheelchair, unable to use her hands. After two years of rehabilitation, she emerged with new skills and a fresh determination to help others in similar situations. Her organization, Joni and Friends, has a variety of programs that serve special-needs families across the U.S. and around the world. Joni authored *Joni: An Unforgettable Story, Place of Healing, Finding God in Hidden Places, Life in the Balance* and many more books.

joniandfriends.org

PAM FARREL

Pam Farrel is an international speaker and author of more than 30 books, including the bestseller *Men Are Like Waffles, Women Are Like*

Spaghetti. Pam and her husband, Bill, are relationship specialists who help people become "love-wise." Pam is also a sought-after women's speaker and encourages women from her books such as *Woman of Influence, The 10 Best Decisions a Woman Can Make,* and *Devotions for Women on the Go.* The Farrels have been happily married for 30 years, and their family includes three children, a daughter-in-law and three grandchildren. The Farrels live in San Diego, California.

love-wise.com
twitter.com/pamfarrel

MARK FOREMAN

 Mark Foreman is the lead pastor at North Coast Calvary Chapel in Carlsbad, California, known for its unique, borderless philosophy of being "a church without walls." He is known internationally as a strategist, conference speaker, church planter, worship leader, published songwriter, counselor and seminary professor. Most recently, he authored *Wholly Jesus.* Mark has spent his life studying the subject of personal and cultural transformation. He holds an undergraduate degree in sociology and religious studies and graduate degrees in theology, counseling and pastoral care. Mark has been married to Jan, his "best friend and favorite Bible teacher," for 39 years. Together they are parents to two grown sons, Jon and Tim, who are part of the band Switchfoot. The Foremans reside in Cardiff, California. Mark's joys are surfing, traveling to under-privileged parts of the world, and spending late hours in the studio with his sons.

northcoastcalvary.org

JENN GOTZON

 Actress Jenn Gotzon's career break was in portraying President Nixon's daughter Tricia Nixon in Ron Howard's Oscar-nominated *Frost/Nixon.* The film launched her as an American leading lady, and she has since starred in several movies (coming soon to theaters). Gotzon, whom *Valley Social Magazine* stated

"is compared to a young Meryl Streep for her chameleon-like transformations," strives to make a difference in people's lives through the roles she plays on and off the screen. Her ultimate passion is impacting and inspiring audiences through the message behind her roles. She developed a motivational mentor-outreach program called Inspiring Audiences, in which she speaks to high school students, screens her movies, and shares her journey on overcoming life's obstacles. Jenn is pursuing her dream to educate and encourage young people on how they, too, can follow their heart's desire and live their dreams.

facebook.com/jenngotzon.fanpage.

NATALIE GRANT

 A powerhouse vocalist, heart-gripping songwriter and charismatic performer, Natalie Grant was the GMA Female Vocalist of the Year for four consecutive years (2006-2009) and the top-selling adult contemporary female solo artist in 2005, 2006 and 2008. Grant is among a select number of artists to have achieved a formidable foothold in mainstream media and radio. Beyond her artistry, she is an outspoken advocate for victims of human trafficking. Abolition International, formerly known as The Home Foundation, which Grant created in 2005, has raised more than a quarter of a million dollars to fight the trafficking of women and children for the purpose of sexual exploitation. She works to balance these endeavors with her greatest calling—as a wife, and mother of three.

nataliegrant.com
facebook.com/nataliegrantmusic
twitter.com/nataliegrant

KENN GULLIKSEN

 After serving four years in the Air Force, Kenn received his Bachelor of Arts degree in Biblical Studies from Southern California College (now Vanguard University). He was privileged to serve as an assistant pastor to Chuck Smith at Calvary Chapel, and then in 1974, with his wife, Joanie, started the first Vine-

yard Christian Fellowship in West Los Angeles. Kenn and Joanie continued to plant and pastor churches for three more decades, and now lead a home church and mentor young leaders. They have four children and four grandchildren.

KIRSTEN HAGLUND

Kirsten Haglund served as Miss America 2008, Goodwill Ambassador for the Children's Miracle Network, spokesperson for the Zerosmoke™ Company, and was a tireless advocate for increased awareness of eating disorders as a public health priority. She founded the Kirsten Haglund Foundation, whose mission is to fundraise to provide treatment scholarships to assist families and individuals battling eating disorders.

kirstenhaglund.org

CYNTHIA HEALD

Cynthia Heald is a popular speaker, ardent fan of A. W. Tozer, and author of the *Becoming a Woman of . . .* Bible studies, which have sold millions of copies. She and her husband, Jack, are full-time staff members with The Navigators in Tucson, Arizona.

cynthiahealdstudies.com

JOHNNY HUNT

Dr. Johnny M. Hunt served as president of the Pastors' Conference of the Southern Baptist Convention in 1996 and as President of the Southern Baptist Convention for the terms 2008-2009 and 2009-2010. Dr. Hunt and his wife, Janet Allen, have two daughters and four grandchildren. He is currently pastor of First Baptist Church, Woodstock, Georgia, hosts an annual Johnny Hunt Men's Conference, and is the author of *Building Your Leadership Resume: Developing the Legacy that Will Outlast You.*

johnnyhunt.com / fbcw.org

STAN JANTZ

Stan Jantz is the publishing director of Regal and the author of more than 50 books, including the million-selling *God Is in the Small Stuff.* Stan is also the co-founder of ConversantLife.com, a popular digital platform that invites meaningful conversations about faith and culture.

conversantlife.com

BILL JOHNSON

Bill Johnson is a fifth-generation pastor with a rich heritage in the Holy Spirit. Together, Bill and his wife serve a growing number of churches that have partnered for revival. This leadership network has crossed denominational lines, building relationships that enable church leaders to walk successfully in both purity and power. Bill and Brenda (Beni) Johnson are the senior pastors of Bethel Church in Redding, California. All three of their children and spouses are involved in full-time ministry. They also have nine wonderful grandchildren. Bill is the author of *When Heaven Invades Earth*, one of the most-read books today helping to shape the next generation of Christians. He also authored *Dreaming With God* and *The Essential Guide to Healing* (with Randy Clark).

ibethel.org
bjm.org

BIANCA JUAREZ

Bianca Juarez is an international Bible teacher, motivational speaker, a frequent college chapel speaker and the director of In the Name of Love Ministries. She is in love with two men: Jesus Christ and her husband, Matt. She enjoys cupcakes, kickboxing and teaching the Word of God—but not necessarily in that order. Bianca and Matt live in Southern California.

inthenameoflove.org

BEN KASICA

Ben Kasica was the lead guitarist for the band Skillet (Atlantic Records/INO) for 10 years. During his time with the band, Skillet sold more than 1.5 million records, was nominated for two Grammy awards, won a Dove Award, and scored numerous #1 radio singles. Ben has run a successful recording business for seven years and has worked with world-renown producers Brian Howes (Hinder, Daughtry, Avril Lavigne, Lifehouse), Paul Ebersold (3 Doors Down, Saliva, Third Day) and Skidd Mills (Saving Abel). He engineered the acoustic bonus tracks on Skillet's *Comatose: Deluxe Edition* album and has co-written and produced music for artists such as Kevin Hammond (A&M/Octone Records), Icon for Hire and Hyland (Tooth & Nail Records). Ben also heads up Life Love Music Clothing and enjoys friends, photography, cooking and sports.

skillet.com

twitter.com/benkasica

DAN KIMBALL

Dan Kimball is on staff at Vintage Faith Church in Santa Cruz, California. The books Dan has authored include *They Like Jesus, But Not The Church; The Emerging Church; Emerging Worship; Listening to the Beliefs of Emerging Churches* and *Sacred Space: A Hands-on Guide to Creating Multisensory Worship Experiences for Youth Ministry* (with Lilly Lewin). He graduated from Colorado State University with a degree in landscape architecture and earned a Master's degree from Western Seminary. He currently serves as an adjunct faculty mentor at George Fox Seminary and is pursuing a Doctor of Ministry degree. He drives a rusty 1966 Mustang and lives in Santa Cruz with his wife, Becky, and their two children, Katie and Claire.

dankimball.com

facebook.com/churchland

twitter.com/dankimball

ESTHER LOVEJOY

Esther Lovejoy was in full-time ministry with the Christian and Missionary Alliance for more than 25 years. She was actively involved in women's ministries both in the local church and on denominational levels. She often spoke at women's retreats and conferences, including citywide events in Akron, Ohio, and Syracuse, New York. Though no longer in full-time ministry, Esther continues to be involved in the lives of women through writing, speaking engagements, personal counseling and Bible studies. She currently has a radio ministry called View from the Sparrow's Nest. Presently, Esther lives in a small town in Pennsylvania with her husband, Peter. Together they share nine children and 18 adorable grandchildren.

viewfromthesparrowsnest.com

TORRY MARTIN

Torry Martin was a standup comic and actor in Los Angeles before he became a Christian. After finding the Lord, Torry moved to Alaska and lived in a remote cabin with a friend who was studying for ministry. He gave up acting and comedy for two years and studied the Bible while becoming grounded in his faith. Torry began writing comedy sketches, which he entered into a national competition sponsored by the Gospel Music Association called Christian Artists (now called Seminar in the Rockies). He won the grand prize two years in a row and now returns annually as an instructor. Martin has written for *Adventures in Odyssey*, a children's radio series produced by Focus on the Family, and now lives in Tennessee.

torrymartin.com

GREGG MATTE

Gregg Matte is the senior pastor of First Baptist Church in Houston, Texas, and is the founder of Breakaway Ministries at Texas A&M University, one of the largest college Bible studies in the nation. He is the author of *The Highest Education: Becoming a Godly Man, Finding God's Will* and *I AM Changes Who I Am,* and is the executive producer of numerous Breakaway praise and worship albums. He is also a popular speaker at conferences, camps and retreats across North America. Gregg has been married to his wife, Kelly, since 1997, and together they have a son, Greyson.

> houstonsfirst.org
> twitter.com/greggmatte

ALEX MCFARLAND

Alex McFarland (M.A., Christian Thought/Apologetics, Liberty University) is a speaker, writer and advocate for Christian apologetics. He is the former president of Southern Seminary and the former director of teen apologetics at Focus on the Family. An author and popular speaker at hundreds of locations throughout the U.S. and abroad, Alex is also the weekly host for the *Truth Talk Live* radio program and the founder of Truth for a New Generation apologetics conferences. He has been interviewed by Billy Graham's *Decision* radio broadcast, James Dobson on Focus on the Family, *The New York Times*, the BBC, *Christianity Today* and many other media outlets. He is the author of *The 10 Most Common Objections to Christianity* and *10 Answers for Skeptics*.

> alexmcfarland.com.

JAMES MEAD

James Mead has been the guitarist for the band Kutless since 2001. The Oregon-based rock band has sold two million records across its first five efforts. Kutless prays that their music not only glorifies God but also impacts listeners in a positive way. James also tweets Tozer quotes.

> kutless.com
> twitter.com/jrmeadkutless

BRITT MERRICK

Britt Merrick grew up immersed in the Southern California surf culture and was the heir to the world's largest surfboard company. After committing his life to Christ in his early twenties, Britt left the family business to teach and preach the Bible and plant churches. He is the founding pastor of the Reality family of churches, which includes locations in Los Angeles, San Francisco, Santa Barbara, Stockton, Carpinteria and London, England. Reality is passionate about church planting, community transformation and equipping and mobilizing the next generation of leaders. Britt is also the author of *Big God*. He lives with his wife and two children near Santa Barbara, California.

brittmerrick.com
facebook.com/pastorbrittmerrick
twitter.com/brittmerrick

CECIL MURPHEY

Veteran author Cecil (Cec) Murphey has written or co-written more than 120 books, including the *New York Times'* bestseller *90 Minutes in Heaven* (with Don Piper) and *Gifted Hands: The Ben Carson Story* (with Dr. Ben Carson). Three of his more recent titles include *When God Turned Off the Lights; Knowing God, Knowing Myself;* and *When a Man You Love Was Abused*. His books have sold in the millions and have given hope and encouragement to countless readers around the world.

cecilmurphey.com

BRITT NICOLE

Britt, a Sparrow Records recording artist and 2011 Dove Female Vocalist nominee, burst onto the Christian music scene in 2007. Since then, she has established herself as a pop-rock mainstay with her deep, honest lyrics and soaring vocals, as evidenced by her #1 debut on the Billboard Top

Christian Albums chart. In 2009, she reached #62 on the Billboard 200 with her sophomore project *The Lost Get Found*. This album, which also delivered hit songs such as "Walk on the Water," "Hanging On" and "Headphones," followed Britt's debut album *Say It*, which also produced three Top 10 radio singles: "You," "Set the World on Fire" and "Believe." Britt's songs have been featured in the major motion picture *Soul Surfer*, LucasArt's *Thrillville 2* video game, the *Legally Blonde 3* DVD, MTV's *The Hills*, NBC's *The Biggest Loser*, Lifetime's *Drop Dead Diva*, ABC Family's *Campus Crush* promo and on the soundtrack for the family-friendly film *Ice Castles*.

> brittnicole.com
> facebook.com/brittnicole
> twitter.com/itsbrittnicole

TONY NOLAN

Tony's passion is "helping people get it about God's great love and salvation"! Recognized among the country's most influential Christian communicators, Tony speaks to more than 800,000 students each year through radio, TV, conferences, festivals, concerts and church events. He recently served as tour pastor and gospel communicator for the Casting Crowns' Lifesong Tour and Winter Jam, the largest Christian concert tour in America. He lives in Woodstock, Georgia, with his wife, Tammy, and their four children, Christy, Wil, Bradly and Joy.

> tonynolan.org

JAMIE OWENS COLLINS

Jamie Owens Collins is an internationally known recording artist, songwriter and public speaker. Her songs include "The Battle Belongs to the Lord" and "The Victor." She has also contributed commentary to *The Worship Bible* and *The Women of Destiny Bible*. Jamie lives in Southern California with her husband, music producer Dan Collins. They have three grown children and two grandchildren.

> fairhillmusic.com

SUSAN PERLMAN

Susan Perlman is one of the founders of Jews for Jesus and serves as their associate executive director. She grew up in a traditional Orthodox Jewish home in Brooklyn, New York, and came to faith in Christ as a young adult. Her testimony is available as a free ebook on their website.

> jewsforjesus.org

LISA ROBSON

Lisa Robson was born and raised in Jacksonville, Florida. She has a passion to see this generation awakened for revival to sweep the nations and has faithfully re-tweeted Tozer quotes (among other inspiring messages) for many years.

> robson21.wordpress.com

DUDLEY RUTHERFORD

Dudley Rutherford is the senior pastor of the 10,000-member Shepherd of the Hills Church in Porter Ranch (Los Angeles), California. He has been honored to serve as the president of the 2011 North American Christian Convention and chapel speaker to several professional sports teams. Dudley's many published works include his breakout book *God Has An App for That*. He resides in Porter Ranch with his wife and three children.

> theshepherd.org/
> callonjesus.com/
> pastordudley.com/
> twitter.com/pastordudley

ABBIE SMITH

Abbie Smith is the author of various books, including *Can You Keep Your Faith in College?* (Multnomah, 2006) and *The Slow Fade* (Cook, 2010). She writes mentoring material and keeps a blog. Abbie resides in Savannah, Georgia, with her husband and best friend, Micah, and their dog, Moses.

xp3college.org
conversantlife.com/blogs/abbie+smith

JUDAH SMITH

Judah and Chelsea Smith are the lead pastors of The City Church in Seattle, Washington. They were the pastors of Generation Church, the youth ministry of The City Church, for 10 years before stepping into their new role in 2009. Judah is the author of several books, including *Dating Delilah*, a book on purity from a new perspective, and also ministers nationally and internationally at churches and conferences, imparting hope into the lives of Christian leaders and young people. His ministry is noted for an anointed, fresh preaching style mixed with humor, authority, passion, and strong faith.

thecity.org
twitter.com/judahsmith

KIMBERLY L. SMITH

Kimberly L. Smith is president and co-founder of Make Way Partners and author of *Passport Through Darkness*. Fighting to end human trafficking in the darkest corners of the world, Kimberly has led the way to building a powerful, indigenously based anti-trafficking network spanning Africa, Eastern Europe and South America. She divides her time between each ministry location and doing writing and public speaking. She lives in Sylacauga, Alabama, with her husband, Milton.

> makewaypartners.org
> kimberlylsmith.com
> twitter.com/lifethatmatters

SCOTT SMITH

Scott Smith is the music director for K-LOVE radio. He has been part of the on-air DJ team Scott and Kelly since 2008 for both K-LOVE and its sister network, Air1 Radio.

> klove.com/
> facebook.com/kloveafternoons
> twitter.com/klovescott

CHARLES R. SWINDOLL

Two passions have directed the life and ministry of Chuck Swindoll: an unwavering commitment to the practical communication and application of God's Word, and an untiring devotion to seeing lives transformed by God's grace. Chuck has devoted more than four decades to these goals, and he models the contagious joy that springs from enthusiastically following Jesus Christ.

> insight.org/
> twitter.com/chuckswindoll

BODIE AND BROCK THOENE

Bodie and Brock Thoene (pronounced *Tay-nee*) have written more than 65 works of historical fiction. These bestsellers have sold more than 25 million copies and won eight ECPA Gold Medallion Awards, affirming what millions of readers have already discovered—that the Thoenes are not only master stylists but also experts at capturing readers' minds and hearts.

In their timeless classic series about Israel (*The Zion Chronicles, The Zion Covenant, The Zion Legacy* and *The Zion Diaries*), the Thoenes' love for both story and research shines. With *The Shiloh Legacy* and *Shiloh Autumn* (poignant portrayals of the American Depression), *The Galway Chronicles* (dramatic stories of the 1840s famine in Ireland), and the *Legends of the West* (gripping tales of adventure and danger in a land without law), the Thoenes have made their mark in modern history. In the *A.D. Chronicles* and the *A.D. Scrolls*, they step seamlessly into the world of Jerusalem and Rome, in the days when Yeshua walked the earth.

Bodie often describes Brock as "an essential half of this writing team." With degrees in both history and education, Brock has, in his role as researcher and storyline consultant, added the vital dimension of historical accuracy. Due to such careful research, the *Zion Covenant, Zion Chronicles, Zion Diaries* and *Zion Legacy* series are recognized by the American Library Association, as well as Zionist libraries around the world, as classic historical novels and are used to teach history in college classrooms.

Bodie and her husband, Brock, have four grown children— Rachel, Jake, Luke and Ellie—and eight grandchildren. Their children are carrying on the Thoene family talent as the next generation of writers. Bodie and Brock divide their time between Hawaii, London and Nevada.

thoenebooks.com/
facebook.com/pages/Bodie-and-Brock-Thoene/10564526
   6134633
twitter.com/bodiethoene

Elmer Towns

Dr. Elmer Towns is a college and seminary professor, an author of popular and scholarly works (the editor of two encyclopedias), a popular seminar lecturer, a dedicated worker in Sunday School, and has developed more than 20 resource packets for leadership education. He co-founded Liberty University with

Jerry Falwell in 1971, and he is the dean of the School of Religion. Dr. Towns and his wife of 55 years, Ruth, live in Forest, Virginia, and have three children and 10 grandchildren.

elmertowns.com/
liberty.edu/
twitter.com/elmertowns

TED TRAVIS

Dr. Ted Travis is a veteran youth leader, having spent more than 30 years unleashing leadership potential among urban youth in northeast Denver. A founding member of the Christian Community Development Association, Ted and his wife, Shelly, reside in Chicago, Illinois, where he serves on the pastoral staff at Lawndale Community Church and continues, through speaking and writing, to advocate for urban youth leadership development.

lawndalechurch.org
ccda.org

BISHOP KENNETH C. ULMER

Dr. Kenneth Ulmer serves as the senior pastor-teacher of Faithful Central Bible Church in Inglewood, California. Under Dr. Ulmer's leadership, Faithful Central Bible Church has grown from 350 people to more than 13,000 since he arrived in 1982. He is an accomplished writer and published author of several books, including *Making Your Money Count* and *Knowing God's Voice*. He is also the presiding bishop of Macedonia International Bible Fellowship. In addition to being a recipient of graduate and doctorate degrees, Dr. Ulmer has contributed through his acts of service to the local community and throughout the world. In his eyes, his greatest success and satisfaction has come as the husband of his wife, Togetta, and the father of their three children. In addition, he has two sons-in-law and five beautiful granddaughters. Dr. Ulmer and Togetta have been married for more than 30 years and currently reside in Los Angeles, California.

faithfulcentral.com/

KRIS VALLOTTON

Kris Vallotton is the senior associate leader of Bethel Church in Redding, California, the co-founder and senior overseer of the Bethel School of Supernatural Ministry, and the founder and president of Moral Revolution, an organization dedicated to cultural transformation. He has written seven books, including the bestselling *Supernatural Ways of Royalty*, *Heavy Rain* and *The Supernatural Power of Forgiveness* (with Jason Vallotton). Kris and Kathy Vallotton have been happily married for 36 years and have four children and eight grandchildren.

kvministries.com/
ibethel.org/
facebook.com/kvministries
twitter.com/kvministries

TOMMY WALKER

Tommy has led worship at Christian Assembly in Los Angeles, California, with his pastor, Mark Pickerill, since 1990. He has traveled with Promise Keepers, Greg Laurie Harvest Crusades and Franklin Graham. He has recorded worship projects for Maranatha! Music, Integrity Music, and Get Down Ministries. Tommy has been married to his wife, Robin, for more than 20 years. They have four children: Jake, Levi, Emmie and Eileen. His greatest achievement will always be to be found faithful to his God and his local church.

tommywalker.net/
facebook.com/tommywalker1
twitter.com/tommy_walker

KURT WARNER

Kurt Warner is a former NFL quarterback who played for the St. Louis Rams, New York Giants and Arizona Cardinals. He was a four-time Pro Bowl selection, two-time AP NFL MVP, a three-time Super Bowl participant and MVP for the Super Bowl XXXIV champion Rams. He is the author of three books and founder of the charitable organization First Things First.

kurtwarner.org
facebook.com/kurt13warner
twitter.com/kurt13warner

ROBERT WHITT

 Bob and Stacy Whitt are senior pastors of Family Life Church. They are under the spiritual covering of Rick Joyner and MorningStar Ministries, in Fort Mill, South Carolina. Pastor Bob has been a catalyst in the unity of churches of various denominations and has been influential in changing the spiritual atmosphere in the region. Bob is pastor of Lauren Barlow's home church.

morningstarministries.org/

BRUCE WILKINSON

 Bruce Wilkinson is a popular speaker, bestselling author, leader of various global and humanitarian causes, and media producer. He has written more than 60 books in 30 languages, including several books that reached the #1 spot on the bestseller lists of *The New York Times*, *Wall Street Journal*, and *USA Today*. *The Prayer of Jabez* was the first book in history to win "Book of the Year" two years in a row, and *Publisher's Weekly* reported that it was the "fastest selling book of all time" (2001).

Bruce's book *A Life God Rewards* was the only religious nonfiction book to hit the #1 spot on the *New York Times* bestseller list in its first week. He is also the *New York Times* bestselling author for children and teen books and the publisher and executive editor of 10 monthly magazines with more than 120,000,000 distributed. Bruce has served on the overview committee of the *New King James Version* of the Bible, has authored the outlines of the books of the Bible for the bestselling *Open Bible,* and is the executive editor of three Bibles.

In addition to *The Prayer of Jabez* and *A Life God Rewards,* he has written *Secrets of the Vine, Beyond Jabez, Set Apart, Experiencing Spiritual Breakthroughs* and *The Dream Giver.* Bruce is married to Darlene and has three children and six grandchildren. The Wilkinsons reside in South Carolina.

brucewilkinson.com
facebook.com/lastinglifechange
twitter.com/bruce_wilkinson

RAVI ZACHARIAS

Ravi Zacharias is the founder, chairman and CEO of Ravi Zacharias International Ministries (RZIM). Through evangelism, undergirded by apologetics, RZIM seeks to reach those who shape the ideas of a culture with the credibility of the gospel of Jesus Christ. Dr. Zacharias is the author of more than 20 books, and his radio programs, *Let My People Think* and *Just Thinking,* are aired on stations worldwide.

rzim.org
facebook.com/pages/ravi-zacharias/42463176812
twitter.com/ravizacharias

DARLENE ZSCHECH

Darlene Zschech is an acclaimed singer, songwriter, worship leader and speaker, most notably for her involvement in the music from Hillsong Church, Sydney. Although she has achieved numerous gold albums and her songs are sung in many nations of the world, her success simply stands as a testimony to her life's passion to serve God and people with all her heart. Today, Darlene and her husband, Mark, are the senior pastors of Hope Unlimited Church on the Central Coast of New South Wales, Australia.

As a songwriter, Darlene is perhaps most famous for the chorus "Shout to the Lord," which was nominated as album of the year for the 1997 Dove Awards and song of the year for the 1998 Dove Awards. Darlene has been nominated songwriter of the year and has received an international award for influence in praise and worship. In addition to "Shout to the Lord," Darlene has written more than 80 songs published by Hillsong. Darlene and Mark have supported the work of Compassion International and initiated Hope: Rwanda, which has now expanded to Cambodia and beyond. Today, Darlene and Mark live on the Central Coast with their three daughters, Chloe, Zoe and Amy, son-in-law Andrew, their beautiful granddaughter, Ava Pearl, and their handsome new grandson, Roman Emmanuel Mark.

darlenezschech.com
hoperwanda.org
twitter.com/darlenezschech

Thank You
from Lauren Barlow

Jesus—You're the love of my life. How would I survive without You.

Dad—Your name should be right next to mine on the cover of this book. I literally couldn't have done it without you.

Mom—Thank you for always believing in me and being my loudest cheerleader in all I do.

Becca and Lyssa, my best friends in this whole world—For encouraging me to do this project and being there for me every step of the way. Now we should probably go practice . . .

Josh, Sabrina, Caleb, Emma, Josie, Tess, and Clara—You are all the sunshine in my life. I cherish you all more than you will ever know.

Beka—I like your baby books . . . and your bagel . . .

Sarah—Let's go eat chocolate and talk about boys. . . . We will never grow up will we?

Danette—You're the reason this book happened, because I couldn't have done it without Microsoft® Word now, could I?

Neenah—Can't believe that you've stuck with me since the "lame" table in kindergarten. I'm so honored to call you friend.

Steven Lawson and Regal—For believing that this drummer from a rock band could edit such an incredible book! Thank you for this amazing opportunity. It's an experience I will never forget.

Shea Vailes—For all your work and keeping everything together! We would have been lost without your organizational skills.

The lovely men and women who wrote for this book—Reading your stories has impacted my life, and I know they will impact everyone who picks up this book. It was an honor to have you as part of this.

BarlowGirl fans—Your support and love over the last 10 years have been unbelievable! You guys are fantastic.

Twitter—For getting me this book deal in the first place.

And what would a book be without all the people behind the scenes! Without all of you this never would have happened! A heartfelt thank you to . . .

Alexis Spencer-Byers and Rebecca English—for your editorial assistance.

Rob Williams—for your inspiring cover and interior design.

Mark Weising—for keeping everyone on schedule!

James Snyder—for providing the original Tozer-Grams and for your inspiring biography of Tozer.

Ken Paton and Wingspread Publications—for keeping Tozer's message alive and allowing us to use so many quotes in this book.

Alison Trowbridge, Stan Jantz and Kathy Helmers—for connecting us with great contributors who are passionate about the message of A.W. Tozer

Wayne Stiles, Jenna Anderson, J. J. Cozzens, Beth Chiles, Mary Berck, Amy Fogleman, Angie Merrill, Carly Barron, Christy Adams, Danielle DuRant, Jenni Burke, Katelyn Rollins, Kyle Griner, Whitney Milton, Stephanie Bennett, Kristi Brazell and Ruth Blakney—for your part in making this book happen.

TO CONNECT WITH LAUREN BARLOW
LOG ON AT

BARLOWGIRL.COM
FACEBOOK.COM/BARLOWGIRL
TWITTER.COM/LAURENABARLOW

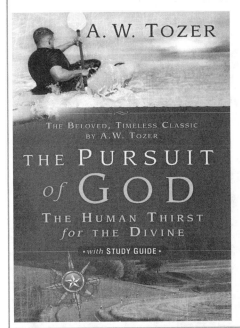
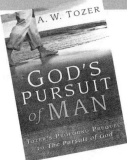

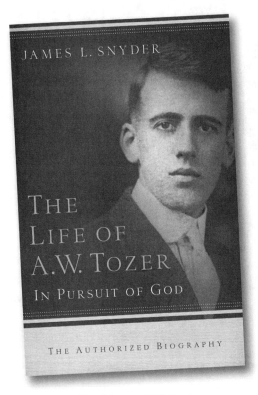

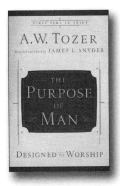
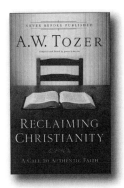
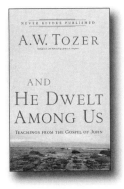
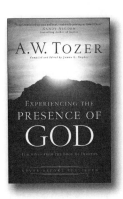
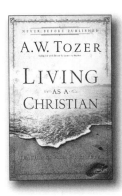
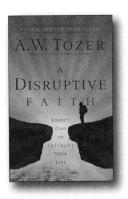